Just starting your Inside Music journey?

If so, you may be interested to know that we can offer on-site training for staff, to complement this new resource.

Voices Foundation training benefits those taking part by:

- developing their personal music skills and knowledge
- boosting their personal confidence when teaching music to children
- expanding their repertoire of music, teaching ideas and strategies
- developing broader teaching skills across the curriculum
- sharing professional development as a team, which fosters a strong sense of community

In turn, their new-found music teaching skills help children:

- find their singing voice and acquire the language of music, through ongoing, structured learning
- develop intellect and character, which in turn boosts their confidence and self esteem
- acquire self-discipline, social skills, communication capabilities and a deep awareness of others

Many judge it to have a positive effect on numeracy and literacy skills, too.

You can opt for as little or as much training as you feel is needed… from a short introductory workshop to help users navigate through the book, right through to a year-long mini-programme, featuring INSETS and one-to-one mentoring and support.

If you'd like to find out more and discuss the possibilities, please complete and return the form below!

YES PLEASE - I'd like to explore options for on-site training to complement:

- ☐ *Early Years*
- ☐ *First Steps: Age 5-7*
- ☐ *First Steps: Age 7-11*
- ☐ All resources

My preferred method of contact is via phone / email / letter (please delete as applicable)

Name	
Job title	
Organisation	
Address	
	Postcode
Telephone	
Email	

Please return by post to: The Voices Foundation
34 Grosvenor Gardens
London SW1W 0DH

Or fax a copy to: 020 7259 0598

Published by The Voices Foundation and Alfred Publishing Co
© The Voices Foundation 2014

Published by The Voices Foundation and Alfred Publishing Co
© The Voices Foundation 2014

Inside Music

A Music Education Programme for Class Teaching (Preschool to Age 13)

First Steps: Age 5-7

Andrew Maddocks

the voices foundation
transforming children through singing

Published by The Voices Foundation and Alfred Publishing Co
© The Voices Foundation 2014

Inside Music

Music confirms our understanding that there is something beyond ourselves. It promotes high-level intellectual and physical attainment, and evokes deep emotional and aesthetic response. It stimulates processes of thinking which require high levels of accuracy and precision. In a unique way, involvement in music provides a rich variety of opportunities for acquiring and developing a wide range of the musical, personal and social skills which our modern world needs.

Music in education is sometimes considered to be little more than enrichment, entertainment or a source of instant gratification. But a deeper interaction with music leads us to appreciate its great beauty and helps us to develop our horizons. It is not simply about learning a body of knowledge. Indeed, music is a wonderful medium for facilitating communication between people of different cultures, ages and social backgrounds.

It follows, therefore, that any music education programme must include first-hand experience of these deeper qualities so that the social, interpersonal and aesthetic benefits of music take up a key position in the way we live our lives.

To achieve these objectives, a music education programme must also have cognitive benefits. It is only when we get 'inside' music that we become aware of the skills, concepts and levels of understanding needed to come to terms fully with the functions of music and the ways in which it is created and assembled.

Inside Music is a core programme designed for teachers and practitioners – both with and without specialist music knowledge – who work with children from birth to age 13. Its current stages are as follows:

■ ***Early Years: To Age 5***
(Handbook/CD: published)

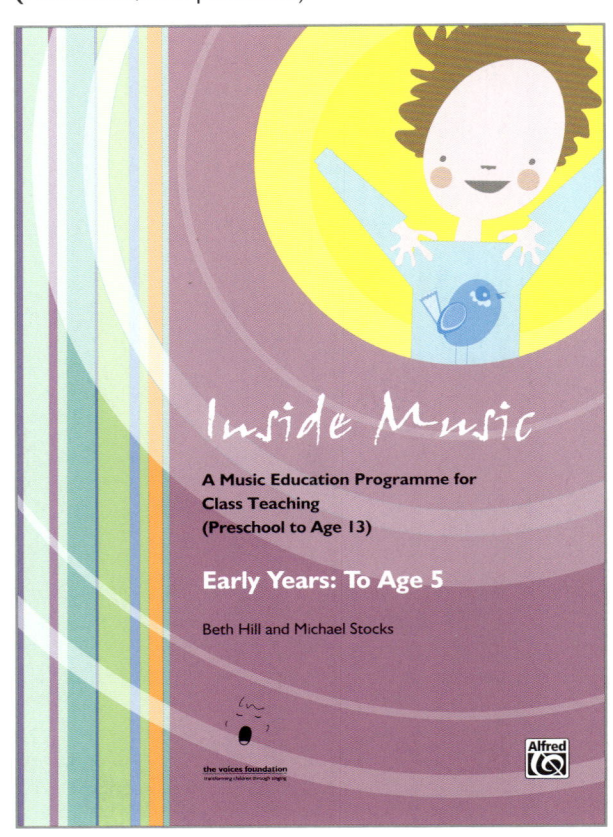

Written by Beth Hill, this handbook provides a range of opportunities to help babies and under-5s to become comfortable with music activity, and to begin to experience some of the music basics by planting seeds for healthy growth in skills and knowledge in music education.

- *First Steps: Age 5-7*
  (Handbook/CD: published)

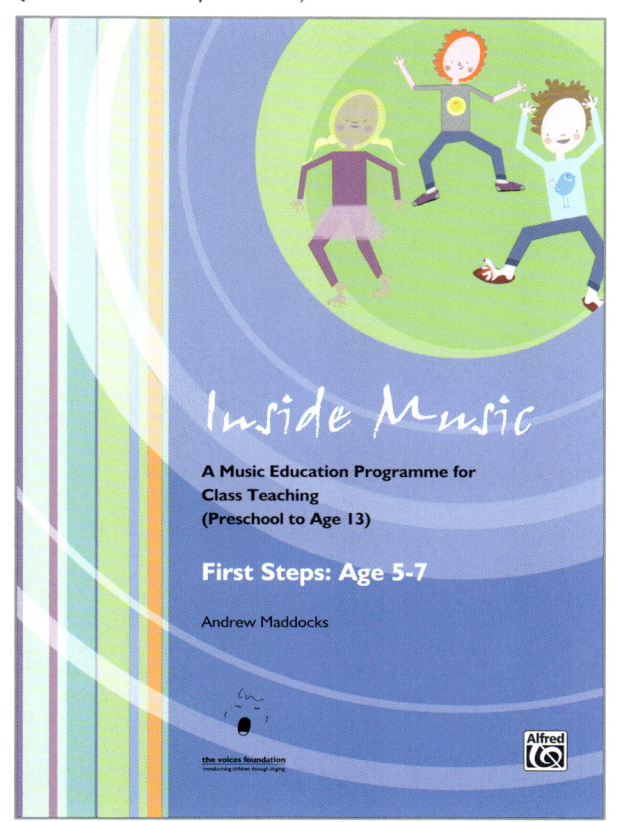

- *First Steps: Age 7-11*
  (Handbook/CD: available from September 2014)

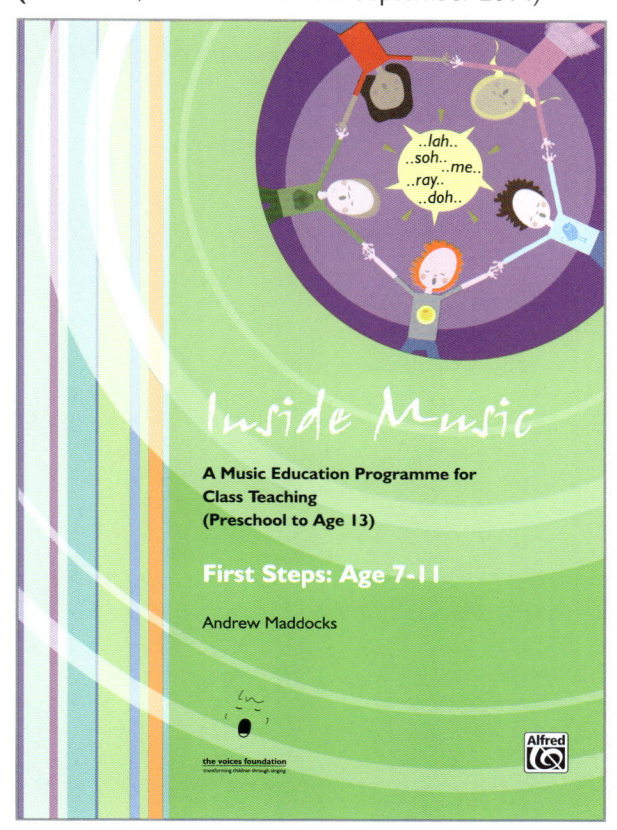

Written by Andrew Maddocks, this handbook is designed for teachers working with children aged between 5 and 7, and is the recommended starting point for this age range.

Written by Andrew Maddocks, this handbook is intended for teachers working with children aged 7 to 11, who are new to the teaching methods featured in *Inside Music*. It is therefore recommended as the entry level for older children across this entire age ran.

Also under development:

- *Second Steps: Age 7-11*
  For teaching older children who have worked through the appropriate introductory handbooks already shown. Recommended for use by music specialists in the main.

- The series will be completed by a *KS3 resource*.

Michael Stocks
Education Consultant, The Voices Foundation

Acknowledgements

Our deepest gratitude goes to Michael Stocks, the creator of The Voices Foundation's methodology, who, since 2008, has worked to create the detailed concept of *Inside Music*, from which **First Steps: Age 5-7** has been drawn.

We are grateful to our colleagues below for their advice and support in creating **First Steps: Age 5-7**.

Consultative Group

Michael Stocks
Sally Cathcart
Suzi Digby (Lady Eatwell) OBE
Beth Hill
Sue Hollingworth
Rosemary Jones
Dame Sylvia Morris
Liz Rayment-Pickard
Nicola Wallis

Proof Readers

Marcia Bennie
Caroline Sindall
Sarah Coatsworth

Illustrator

Chris Wright

CD Production/Singers

Beth Hill
Sarah Carling
Jan Trott

Designer

Tracy Miles, Somerton Computing

Independent Advisors

Linda Bruce
Matthew Coatsworth
Selina Smyth

We have made every effort to trace and acknowledge copyright owners. If any of them are not listed below, we offer our apologies and ask that you contact us immediately.

I, I, me oh my from Be a Real Musician –
Geoffry Russell-Smith
© Boosey & Hawkes Music Publishers Ltd 1977

Naxos Licensing

National Youth Choir of Scotland

The Grasshopper's Dance
© Chandos 2004

Clog Dance from La fille mal gardée No. 17a
© Decca/Universal 1962

La Toupie from Jeux d'enfants Op. 22
© Decca 2003

Published by The Voices Foundation and Alfred Publishing Co
© The Voices Foundation 2014

Contents

First Steps: Age 5-7	6
Planning For Music	9
The Teaching Programme	23
The Songs	115
Teaching Extras	155
The CD	165

First Steps: Age 5-7

First Steps: Age 5-7 is a handbook for teachers working with young children in their early school career, and forms part of the **Inside Music** programme. The intention of the handbook is to provide a practical guide for teaching music to children over a two-year period, equating to Key Stage 1 in the English education system. It aims to establish confidence in both teacher and children, and to begin to secure a progression of teaching and learning.

Central to the teaching process is performing. Performing gives the child the essential tactile experience of being 'inside music'. At the very heart of the performing experience is the emotional experience of singing. It is a collective and personal experience, one to be shared and enjoyed with friends around you. This programme makes no apology for singing being the dominant performing medium at this stage of the child's musical education.

Performing also includes body action and movement and the playing of instruments. To an extent the two are related, the instrument being an extension of the body. The approach to instruments, however, ought to have respect for those things that will enable progression of skills and control ease of handling, fundamental percussive techniques and instrument care. **First Steps: Age 5-7** introduces these aspects of percussion playing.

Singing is made possible by hearing, the voice, memory and response; it is the result of brain working with living tissue; it is the result of human contact and human need. Therefore it is most natural that singing should be the core of music experience and music teaching.

Singing is a human instrument to be 'found', fostered and developed. To achieve this, the singer needs to 'discover' the Singing Voice, gaining confidence and an ability to sing as an individual, acquire those habits that make voice development possible, and prime the aural memory with music that will be drawn upon for developing skills and concepts.

Listening and thinking will be at the centre of performing, but it is an activity that has several branches: there is listening to the teacher who will be passing on songs to the children; there is listening to others, children, adults, recordings; there is the inner voice that works with the memory, the Thinking Voice; there are the finer skills of discrimination - distinguishing one sound from another, making decisions about how a song is to be sung. It is also worth remembering the importance that listening and thinking have in the development of other areas of learning, eg reading and spelling.

The understanding of music concepts follows naturally from minds that have received a suitable and balanced repertoire of songs. The choice of our songs is not haphazard or based on a whim or popular sentiment. Our chosen songs are ones to which children can relate. Indeed, most in this handbook stem from the playground with activities that children see as games, or having subjects with which they easily associate. But, importantly, the songs have to be carefully selected to enable the child to learn new skills and acquire knowledge.

The concepts of music – phrase, rhythm, pitch etc. – are readily grasped when there is first a useful and relevant platform of practical experience. When the performing experiences are appropriate, then understanding and knowledge about music will follow.

First Steps: Age 5-7 offers structure, progression, teaching ideas, songs and recorded music; it offers these to all teachers who wish to give children the best start to their musical education. It sees things from two perspectives: the potential of children, and the challenge to realise that potential through you, the teacher. It has been written with the intention of being as user-friendly as possible.

First Steps: Age 5-7 is a two-dimensional tool for a three-dimensional activity. Only the practitioner or the teacher can take the songs and teaching ideas off the page and bring them to life for the children. There is no substitute for the personal and 'live' interaction between you and the child. Of course there can be professional support from colleagues, and please bear in mind that complementary training is offered by The Voices Foundation.

Andrew Maddocks
Editor, First Steps: Age 5-7
Senior Adviser, The Voices Foundation

Planning For Music

The Stepping Stones

30 progressive steps of skills and concepts

Units 1 – 16 [Year 1]

Let's start

Unit 1
Listening and performing
- Listening to teacher
- Imitating song phrases

Unit 2
Performing: singing
- Finding the Singing Voice
- Pitch matching
- Individual singing

Unit 9
Concept: timbre
- Voices
- Instruments

Unit 8
Performing: playing
- Percussion sound

Unit 10
Performing: singing
- One breath per phrase
- Sound quality

Unit 11
Listening and thinking
- Recognising song melody

Unit 12
Performing: singing and playing
- Rhythmic speech and tapping
- Actions felt as pulse
- Rhythm on percussion

Unit 13
Concept: phrase
- Start and end

Published by The Voices Foundation and Alfred Publishing Co
© The Voices Foundation 2014

Unit 3
Listening and thinking
- Recorded sound
- Voiced sound

Unit 4
Performing: singing
- Songs and games
- Higher - lower pitch

Unit 5
Listening and thinking
- Recognising known song melody

Unit 6
Performing: singing
- Starting-pitch control
- Wider pitch-range songs
- Dynamics control

Unit 7
Listening and thinking
- Finding the Thinking Voice

Onwards to Year 2

Unit 15
Listening and thinking
- Internalising rhythmic and melodic phrases

Unit 14
Concepts: dynamics, pitch, tempo
- Louder - quieter [dynamics]
- Higher - lower [pitch]
- Faster - slower [tempo]

Unit 16
Concept: rhythm
- Simple time rhythm
- Speaking-names *ta teh-teh*

The Stepping Stones

30 progressive steps of skills and concepts

Units 17 – 30 [Year 2]

Unit 27
Concept: rhythm
- Simple time notation
- Reading and writing

Unit 26
Performing: singing
- Controlling a song's starting-pitch

Unit 25
Concept: tempo
- Relation of pulse to speed

Unit 24
Performing: percussion
- Technique
- Louder/quieter

Unit 23
Concept: phrase
- Same/different
- Length

Year 2 starts here

Unit 18
Concept: metre
- 4-beat metre

Unit 17
Listening and thinking
Concept: pitch
- Demonstrating pitch changes
- Melodic shape
- Rise and fall

Unit 28
Performing: improvising
Concept: pitch
- Melodic phrases using *lah, soh* and *me*
- *lah - soh - me*

Finished!

Unit 30
Performing
Concepts
Listening and thinking
- A reprise

Unit 29
Concept: rhythm
- Simple time: the silent Z

Unit 22
Performing: improvising
- Simple time rhythm phrases

Unit 21
Listening and thinking
- Recorded music: vocal music; longer pieces
- Recognising song melody/rhythm

Unit 19
Performing: imitating
Concept: pitch
- Using *soh* and *me* singing-names
- *soh - me*

Unit 20
Concepts: pulse and rhythm
- Distinguishing

What will you do this term?

- The 30 **Skill and Concept Units** provide the platform for a two-year teaching period; for schools in England, this covers 6 terms of teaching during Years 1 and 2, at Key Stage 1 (approximately 12-13 weeks per term, and a total period of 76 weeks).
- Each **Unit** is the basis for several weeks of music teaching.
- A **Unit** is not a single lesson plan.
- As a guide, with the English education system as a reference point, you could aim to allocate the 30 **Skill and Concept Units** like this:

Year 1

Term 1   1 – 5

Term 2   6 – 10

Term 3   11 – 16

Year 2

Term 4   17 – 21

Term 5   22 – 26

Term 6   27 – 30

- There is a **Unit Checklist** for your convenience on page 24.

How will you allocate time for your music teaching?

- Music performing and listening is a **transient experience**; it exists in time; it starts, it travels, it finishes – and is then only a **memory**.
- This makes music learning very **memory-dependent**.
- A **young memory** is wonderfully agile and capable, but has limited retention span. **Time** fades the **memory** quickly.
- **Skills** in general require **regular practice** if a state of **habit-memory** (instant memory recall) is to be achieved.
- **Music skills** are **aural memory** dependent, but are helped and prompted by associated **muscle memory** and **visual symbols** (notes etc.).
- A strategy of 'little and often' is much the best for this teaching approach.
- **Let's aim for a planned 10 minutes each day - mini-lessons!**

Unit 1
1. **Preparation**
Teaching songs listed for this Unit

Unit 1
2. **Making Conscious**
Raising awareness of Unit's skill/concept through known songs, the teaching ideas and related language

Unit 1
3. **Practice**
Practising & assessing new skill/concept

Unit 2
1. **Preparation**
Revising known songs/teaching new songs listed for this Unit

Unit 2
2. **Making Conscious**
Raising awareness of Unit's skill/concept through known songs, the teaching ideas and related language

Published by The Voices Foundation and Alfred Publishing Co
© The Voices Foundation 2014

How do I get the best out of a Unit?

Each **Unit** consists of **three teaching phases**:

1. **Preparation**: learning new songs and revisiting others
2. **Making Conscious**: teaching the skill or concept
3. **Practice**: reinforcing and assessing new and continuing skills and understanding

During the **Preparation** phase, children acquire <u>vital</u> musical experience in preparation for phase 2 through an in-depth assimilation of the Key Songs.

During the **Making Conscious** phase, children become actively aware of the Unit's skill or concept focus through the songs and Teaching Ideas.

During the **Practice** phase, children are helped to acquire greater skill and understanding; if appropriate, they revisit ongoing skills and concepts in preparation for the next Unit.

- In **reality** the **three phases** will often *overlap* each other.
- The **teaching phases** can be seen graphically below:

Each Unit will state the **Teaching Objectives**, what the activities will focus on and what **Learning Outcomes** can be expected.

- The **Key Songs** are those that are central to the teaching. Each song melody with words is provided with the Unit. The full versions of the songs can be found in The Songs, page 115.
- **Hot Song** is usually a game or action song that could be sung for additional enjoyment; if no song is listed in a particular Unit, you may wish to add your own title.
- **Key Listening** is recorded music on the accompanying CD and provides material for specific teaching ideas and for relaxed listening.
- **Top Tips** provide important guidance for creating teaching success.
- **What Next?** This will often recommend that the teacher revisits with the children a previous Unit for revision of a skill or concept that will be developed in the next Unit.

How long should I spend teaching a Unit?

- Different Units have **different amounts of content**.
- Some Units may take you two weeks; others up to four weeks.
- Much depends on time given to teaching the **Units**.
- A guide to the expectation of **Unit time-length**, based on the recommended **10 minutes-a-day mini-lessons**, can be found against each Unit heading in the Teaching Programme.
- The **teaching ideas** are grouped in **sets**, eg *Set One*.
- The teacher will make the final judgement about time taken to teach a Unit, perhaps with the help of a colleague or the Curriculum Leader.

Unit 2
3. Practice
Practising & assessing new skill/concept

Onwards to Unit 3
or
Optional: Reviewing and adding
Songs, games, honing skills, using known concepts, assessing new skill/concept

What could a teaching plan for Unit 1 look like?

Here is the Unit content:

SKILL AND CONCEPT SEQUENCE
- Listening and performing [two weeks]

TEACHING OBJECTIVES
- To listen to and to imitate song phrases

WHAT IS GOING TO HAPPEN?
- You sing – class listens / class imitates – you listen
- Teaching songs by phrase
- Building a 'Song Bag'

KEY SONGS
Key Songs are known <u>before</u> using Teaching Ideas
Italics = first time appearance
- *Copy me*
- *Hello, how are you?*
- *I, I, me oh my*
- *Rain on the green grass*

HOT SONG

TOP TIPS
- Pointing to oneself = 'I sing'; 'over-to-you' gesture to children = 'you sing'
- Quieter singing improves accuracy, sound quality, confidence
- Young voices prefer singing at a higher pitch
- Sing with facial joy – it's infectious!

TEACHING IDEAS

Set One
- Commit to memory a song from the Key Songs list Sing from memory as class listens
- Repeat above with other songs on other occasions
- Consider a focus for listening, eg *"What does the rain fall on?"* [Rain on the green grass]

Set Two
- Sing phrase 1 from a song as class listens; class imitates as you listen
  - Repeat to aid their memory and accuracy
  - Following phrases are similarly taught
- Sing pairs of consecutive phrases; class imitates Ask *"Who is singing? Who is listening?"*

Set Three
- Starting familiar songs: you sing phrase 1, class repeats and then continues; use gestures to say who should be singing

LEARNING OUTCOMES
- Routine for teaching any new song
- Routine for starting known songs
- The routines help early confidence building and establishing the Singing Voice

WHAT NEXT?
- Move to Unit 2

Before starting

Check the content of the **Unit** to be taught and ask:

- Which songs do I need to learn myself for later teaching?
- Do I need guidance from someone about any aspect?
- Do I need to look at the next Unit to see which songs need to be learnt?

WEEK 1

First Lesson

Focus on **Songs** [Preparation]

Subsequent Lessons

Focus on **Songs** and **Teaching Ideas** [Preparation and Making Conscious]

WEEK 2

First Lesson

Focus on **Songs** and **Teaching Ideas**

Last Lesson

Practice [Reinforcing Assessing]

Focus on **Songs** and **Teaching Ideas** [Making Conscious]

Towards the end of the planned teaching period you will need to decide:

- Whether the Unit aims have been achieved
- Whether the children need more time with the Unit
- Whether you can move on to the next Unit

The weekly plans of Mini-Lessons might look like this

- A blank Planning Template is to be found on page 20 and can be downloaded from the accompanying CD.
- The Units have **Sets** of Teaching Ideas: identify which Sets you will be working with across the suggested number of weeks.
- Note down for each week which songs are going to be covered and any Top Tips or personal reminders needed.
- The following examples show how you might plan the first two Units.

THE VOICES FOUNDATION		FIRST STEPS: AGE 5-7
Year/Term: Autumn 1	Class: Wrens	Teacher: Mr Byrd

Unit No/Focus: 1 – Listening and performing – 2 weeks

Teaching Objectives: To listen to and to imitate song phrases

Week One: Unit 1
Songs: Copy me; Hello, how are you; Rain on the green grass
Listening: –
Teaching: Set 1: teach songs phrases by phrase. REMEMBER to ask questions to focus listening. Use 'I sing-you sing' gestures. MILE!

Week Two: Unit 1 and learning songs for Unit 2
Songs: Rain on the green grass; I, I, me oh my; Have you brought? I see you
Listening: –
Teaching: Set 2: I sing 1st phrase and class listens and then copies – I listen to them. Set 3: I sing 1st phrase and class continues song. REMEMBER GESTURES.

Week Three: Move onto Unit 2
Songs:
Listening:
Teaching:

Week Four:
Songs:
Listening:
Teaching:

Assessment and Comments:
New songs underlined

THE VOICES FOUNDATION			FIRST STEPS: AGE 5-7
Year/Term: Autumn 1	Class: Wrens		Teacher: Mr Byrd
Unit No/Focus: 2 – Performing: singing – 3 weeks		Teaching Objectives: To find the Singing Voice; to sing together at the same pitch; to start to sing individually	

Week One: Unit 2 – Put 3 x 10 mins sessions in timetable
Songs: Have you brought? I see you; Hello, how are you? I, I, me oh my
Listening: –
Teaching: Set 1: Use Have you brought to highlight different voices (speaking, whispering, high, singing, growly, squeaky, choir etc.). Learn other new song and children to invent actions. Play the game for I, I, me oh my as Hot Song!
Week Two: Unit 2
Songs: Have you brought? I see you; Can you tap your shoulders? Hey, hey, look at me; Hello, how are you?
Listening: –
Teaching: Teaching: Start each session with Have you brought? and Hello, how are you? Set 2 – Use the 'Singing Tree' idea to help move pitch around. Maybe draw a tree on the board? Find bird puppet. Encourage confident individuals to model to others. REMEMBER I sing first and need to change the pitch (higher/lower).
Week Three: Unit 2 and learning songs for Unit 3
Songs: Can you tap your shoulders? Tick, tock, see our clock; Who has the penny? Doggie, doggie.
Listening: –
Teaching: Set 3 – Teach Tick, tock in first session of week. In subsequent sessions change hour and starting pitch. Also do this in small groups and give 2/3 individual opportunities each time. Keep this activity short and to the point! Use Singing Tree to help if needed. REMEMBER each session needs a game.
Week Four: Move onto Unit 3
Songs:
Listening:
Teaching:
Assessment and Comments: Change starting pitch of I see you and sing to individual children. Can they match the pitch?

Planning Template

THE VOICES FOUNDATION		FIRST STEPS: AGE 5-7
Year/Term:	Class:	Teacher:

Unit No/Focus:	Teaching Objectives:

Week One:

Songs:

Listening:

Teaching:

Week Two:

Songs:

Listening:

Teaching:

Week Three:

Songs:

Listening:

Teaching:

Week Four:

Songs:

Listening:

Teaching:

Assessment and Comments:

Teaching Extras

Added Bonus Time

- There may be moments in the day when it's time to do something different, or moments that would be well spent having some further learning enjoyment from music-making.

- **Added Bonus Time** – to be found on pages 156–158 – offers you suggested ideas for those moments.

At the drop of a hat!

This is a series of individual ideas in a technically progressive order.

Take a Dip!

This is a progressive and cumulative idea that builds and develops as the children learn more and more songs, and gradually acquire additional musical skills and knowledge.

Listening Material

This aspect is an integral part of the Units and the Teaching Ideas; starting at page 159 there is background information about each piece with a list of its performers that should be helpful to the teacher and of interest to the children.

Keywords

On page 164 there are definitions of the musical terms used in the book's Teaching Programme.

The Teaching Programme

Unit Checklist

PAGE	UNIT	FOCUS	DONE	NOTE
28	1	**Listening and performing** ☐ Listening to teacher ☐ Imitating song phrases		
30	2	**Performing: singing** ☐ Finding the Singing Voice ☐ Pitch matching ☐ Individual singing		
33	3	**Listening and thinking** ☐ Recorded sound ☐ Voiced sound		
35	4	**Performing: singing** ☐ Songs and games ☐ Higher - lower pitch		
38	5	**Listening and thinking** ☐ Recognising known song melody		
41	6	**Performing: singing** ☐ Starting-pitch control ☐ Wider pitch-range songs ☐ Dynamics control		
44	7	**Listening and thinking** ☐ Finding the Thinking Voice		
47	8	**Performing: playing** ☐ Percussion sound		

PAGE	UNIT	FOCUS	DONE	NOTE
49	9	**Concept: timbre** ☐ Voices ☐ Instruments		
51	10	**Performing: singing** ☐ One breath per phrase ☐ Sound quality		
54	11	**Listening and thinking** ☐ Recognising song melody		
57	12	**Performing: singing and playing** ☐ Rhythmic speech and tapping ☐ Actions felt as pulse ☐ Rhythm on percussion		
60	13	**Concept: phrase** ☐ Start and end		
63	14	**Concepts: dynamics, pitch, tempo** ☐ Louder - quieter [dynamics] ☐ Higher - lower [pitch] ☐ Faster - slower [tempo]		
66	15	**Listening and thinking** ☐ Internalising rhythmic and melodic phrases		
69	16	**Concept: rhythm** ☐ Simple time rhythm ☐ Speaking-names *ta* *teh-teh*		

PAGE	UNIT	FOCUS	DONE	NOTE
72	17	**Listening and thinking** **Concept: pitch** ■ Demonstrating pitch changes ■ Melodic shape ■ Rise and fall		
75	18	**Concept: metre** ■ 4-beat metre		
78	19	**Performing: imitating** **Concept: pitch** ■ Using *soh* and *me* singing-names ■ *soh - me*		
81	20	**Concepts: pulse and rhythm** ■ Distinguishing		
84	21	**Listening and thinking** ■ Recorded music: vocal music; longer pieces ■ Recognising song melody/rhythm		
87	22	**Performing: improvising** ■ Simple time rhythm phrases		
90	23	**Concept: phrase** ■ Same/different ■ Length		
93	24	**Performing: percussion** ■ Technique ■ Louder/quieter		

PAGE	UNIT	FOCUS	DONE	NOTE
96	25	**Concept: tempo** ■ Relation of pulse to speed		
98	26	**Performing: singing** ■ Controlling a song's starting-pitch		
101	27	**Concept: rhythm** ■ Simple time notation ■ Reading and writing		
104	28	**Performing: improvising** **Concept: pitch** ■ Melodic phrases using *lah*, *soh* and *me* ■ *lah - soh - me*		
107	29	**Concept: rhythm** ■ Simple time: the silent Z		
110	30	**Performing: singing, playing, improvising** **Concepts: dynamics, phrase, pitch, pulse, rhythm, tempo, timbre** **Listening and thinking** ■ *First Steps: Age 5-7 – a reprise*		

Unit 1

Two weeks

SKILL AND CONCEPT SEQUENCE
- Listening and performing

TEACHING OBJECTIVES
- To listen to and to imitate song phrases

WHAT IS GOING TO HAPPEN?
- You sing – class listens / class imitates – you listen
- Teaching songs by phrase
- Building a 'Song Bag'

KEY SONGS
Key Songs are known *before* using Teaching Ideas
Italics = first time appearance
- *Copy me*
- *Hello, how are you?*
- *I, I, me oh my*
- *Rain on the green grass*

HOT SONG

TOP TIPS
- Pointing to oneself = 'I sing'; 'over-to-you' gesture to children = 'you sing'
- Quieter singing improves accuracy, sound quality, confidence
- Young voices prefer singing at a higher pitch
- Sing with facial joy – it's infectious!

TEACHING IDEAS

Set One
- Commit to memory a song from the Key Songs list Sing from memory as class listens
- Repeat above with other songs on other occasions
- Consider a focus for listening, eg *"What does the rain fall on?"* [Rain on the green grass]

Set Two
- Sing phrase 1 from a song as class listens; class imitates as you listen
  - Repeat to aid their memory and accuracy
  - Following phrases are similarly taught
- Sing pairs of consecutive phrases; class imitates Ask *"Who is singing? Who is listening?"*

Set Three
- Starting familiar songs: you sing phrase 1, class repeats and then continues; use gestures to say who should be singing

LEARNING OUTCOMES
- Routine for teaching any new song
- Routine for starting known songs
- The routines help early confidence building and establishing the Singing Voice

WHAT NEXT?
- Move to Unit 2

COPY ME — TRACK 9

Co-py me, co-py me, You can do it too! Co-py me, co-py me, Then I'll co-py you.

HELLO, HOW ARE YOU? — TRACK 20

Hel - lo, how are you? Ve - ry well, thank - you.

Published by The Voices Foundation and Alfred Publishing Co
© The Voices Foundation 2014

Unit 1

I, I, ME OH MY — TRACK 32

I, I, me oh my, how I like my ap-ple pie.

RAIN ON THE GREEN GRASS — TRACK 48

Rain on the green grass, Rain on the tree.
Rain on the roof-top, but not on me.

hello, how are you?

Unit 2

Three weeks

SKILL AND CONCEPT SEQUENCE
- Performing: singing

TEACHING OBJECTIVES
- To find the Singing Voice
- To sing collectively at the same pitch
- To start to sing as individuals

WHAT IS GOING TO HAPPEN?
- Singing within a group
- Singing as a group at the same pitch
- Singing as an individual within group activities

KEY SONGS
Key Songs are known *before* using Teaching Ideas
Italics = first time appearance
- *Can you tap your shoulders?*
- *Have you brought?*
- Hello, how are you?
- *Hey, hey, look at me*
- *I see you*
- *Tick, tock, see our clock*

HOT SONG

TOP TIPS
- Standing – or sitting on *chairs* – is vital for 'tuneful' singing
- Hearing *himself* helps the child discover and improve
- Sometimes a child can be an effective singing model for the class or an individual to imitate
- Reminder: for secure collective song-start, you sing phrase 1 before children join in

TEACHING IDEAS

Set One
'Have you brought?'
- Class discovers what the voice can do – see The Songs section

'I see you'
- Echo song for pairs
- you + class
- you + child
- child + you
- child + child
- child + class

Set Two
'Hello, how are you?'
- Play 'Hide 'n' seek' in the imaginary 'Singing Tree'
- You sing question, class sings answer: to 'find' you they *must* sing at your pitch
- You sing question at a different pitch level: can they match and 'find' you?
- On repeats higher / lower / even higher: can class 'find' your pitch?
- Use 'Can you tap your shoulders?' in similar way

Set Three
'Tick, tock, see our clock'
- Agree an hour, eg 10 o'clock; you sing phrase 1, class sings phrase 2
- Change the hour … change the singing pitch …
- Phrase 2 can be sung by a group / pair / individual

'Hey, hey, look at me'
- Child selects action and <u>leads</u> the song; class imitates

Assessing Activity
'I see you'
- Teaching Ideas *Set One*

Unit 2

LEARNING OUTCOMES
- Children are 'finding' or have 'found' their Singing Voices
- Children can usually match the selected pitch for a song
- Confidence is being established for individual singing

WHAT NEXT?
- Revisit Unit 1 songs to help memory
- Move to Unit 3

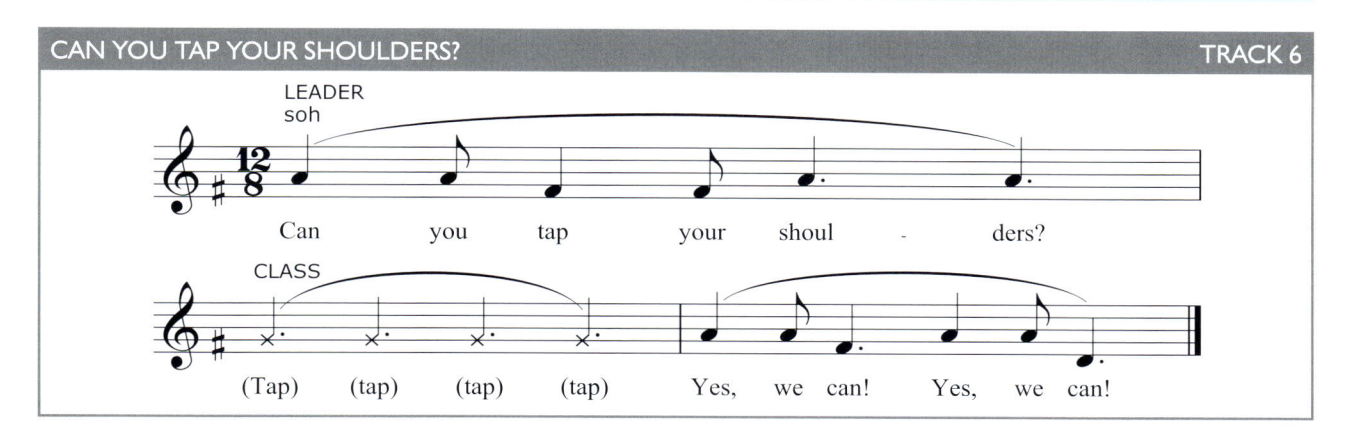

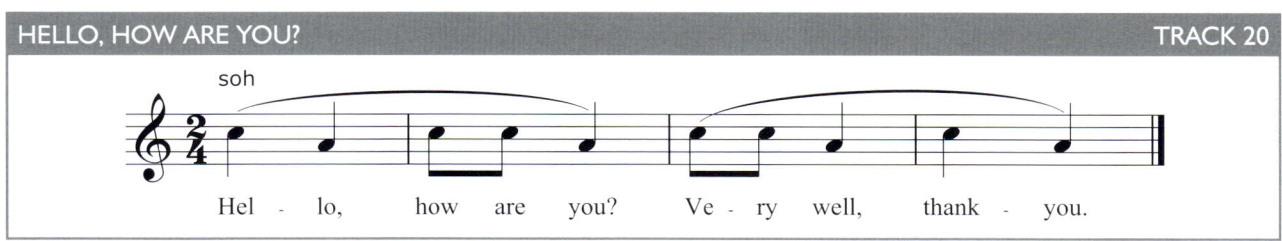

CAN YOU TAP YOUR SHOULDERS? — TRACK 6

LEADER
soh
Can you tap your shoul - ders?

CLASS
(Tap) (tap) (tap) (tap) Yes, we can! Yes, we can!

HAVE YOU BROUGHT? — TRACK 19

CALL
Have you brought your speak-ing voice?

RESPONSE
Yes, we have! Yes, we have!

Have you brought your whis-p'ring voice? Yes, we have! Yes, we have!

soh
Have you brought your sing-ing voice? Yes, we have! Yes, we have!

HELLO, HOW ARE YOU? — TRACK 20

soh
Hel - lo, how are you? Ve - ry well, thank - you.

Published by The Voices Foundation and Alfred Publishing Co
© The Voices Foundation 2014

Unit 2

HEY, HEY, LOOK AT ME — TRACK 27

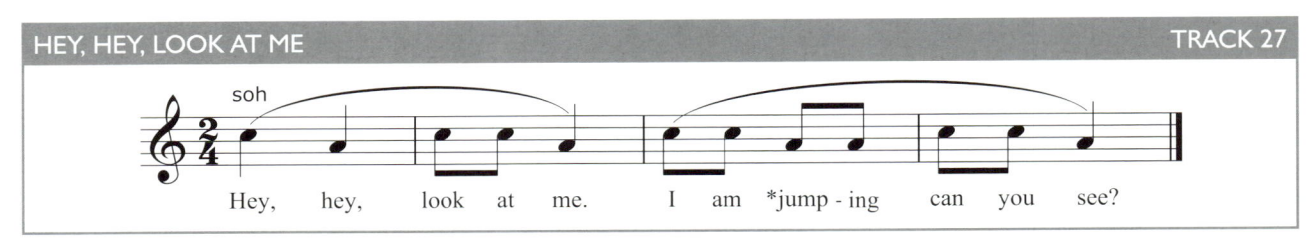

Hey, hey, look at me. I am *jump-ing can you see?

I SEE YOU — TRACK 33

I see you. I see you.
How do you do? How do you do?

TICK, TOCK, SEE OUR CLOCK — TRACK 58

Tick, tock, tick, tock, see our clock.
Tick, tock, tick, tock, twelve o' clock.

Unit 3

Two/three weeks

SKILL AND CONCEPT SEQUENCE
- Listening and thinking

TEACHING OBJECTIVES
- To listen attentively to recorded sound
- To recognise individual voices

WHAT IS GOING TO HAPPEN?
- Class hears recorded music with a specific focus
- Class identifies individuals from their singing

KEY SONGS
Key Songs are known *before* using Teaching Ideas
Italics = first time appearance
- *Doggie, doggie*
- *Jelly on a plate*
- *Who has the penny?*

Key Listening
- The Grasshopper's Dance
- Le Coucou

HOT SONG
- Hickety tickety

TOP TIPS
- Make a 'Song Tree' collage on which known song titles are hung
- A smiley face helps those looking for their voice

TEACHING IDEAS

Set One

Listening 'The Grasshopper's Dance'
- Play about 40 seconds, can class hear the grasshoppers jumping and their 'chirruping' sound? Repeat and fingers dance when the sound is heard
- The piece might be a stimulus for a 'mini-beast' project

Listening 'Le Coucou' [The cuckoo]
- Hear the busy cuckoo flying and calling from all over the wood

Set Two

'Who has the penny?'
- See The Songs section for activities

'Doggie, doggie'
- See The Songs section for activities

'Jelly on a plate'
- Two children speak rhyme together; out of sight only one chants rhyme
  'Who was it?'

Class remembers rhymes and songs
- Make a list
- Individually three children select one without saying which
- Out of sight the three in turn chant or sing
  'Who was first, second and third?'

Assessing Activity

'Doggie, doggie'
- Use the game activity

'Jelly on a plate'
- Use the *Set Two* activity but a child is invited to answer *'Who was it?'*

LEARNING OUTCOMES
- Children are aware that sound can help them identify creatures and humans
- Children listen more acutely when no visual image is present

WHAT NEXT?
- Move to Unit 4

Published by The Voices Foundation and Alfred Publishing Co
© The Voices Foundation 2014

Unit 3

DOGGIE, DOGGIE — TRACK 10

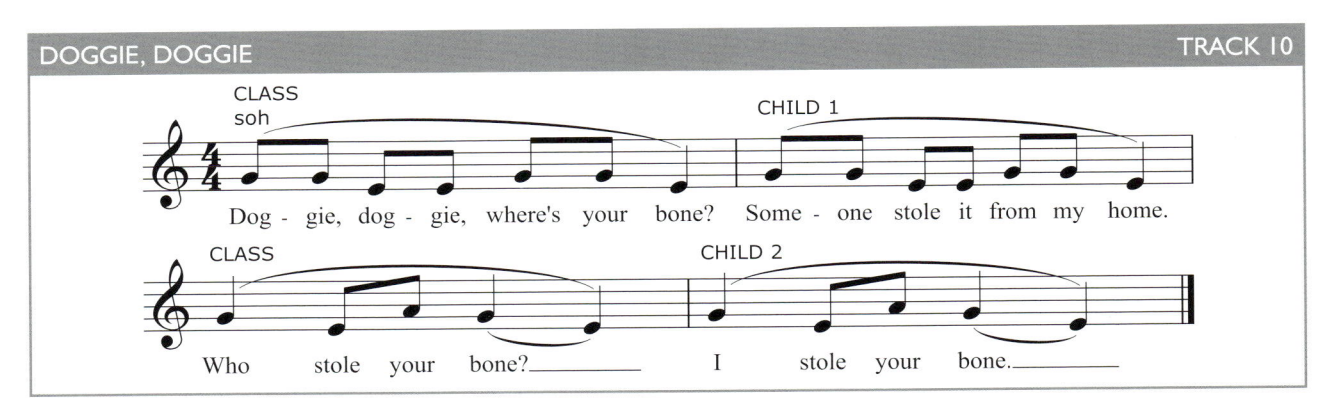

CLASS (soh): Dog-gie, dog-gie, where's your bone?
CHILD 1: Some-one stole it from my home.
CLASS: Who stole your bone?
CHILD 2: I stole your bone.

JELLY ON A PLATE — TRACK 36

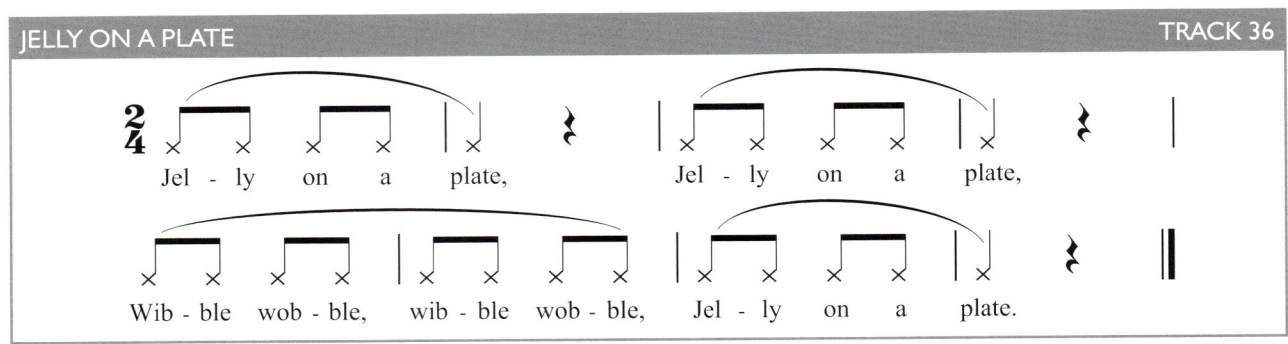

Jel-ly on a plate, Jel-ly on a plate,
Wib-ble wob-ble, wib-ble wob-ble, Jel-ly on a plate.

WHO HAS THE PENNY? — TRACK 60

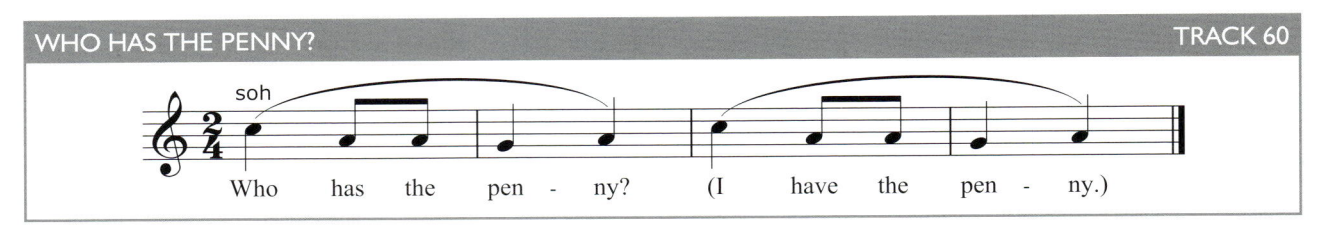

(soh) Who has the pen-ny? (I have the pen-ny.)

Unit 4

Two weeks

SKILL AND CONCEPT SEQUENCE
- Performing: singing

TEACHING OBJECTIVES
- Individuals to take on the role of leader
- To raise children's awareness of pitch

WHAT IS GOING TO HAPPEN?
- Singing game songs requiring a leader
- Class experiences songs and activities fostering awareness of higher and lower pitch levels

KEY SONGS
Key Songs are known *before* using Teaching Ideas
Italics = first time appearance

Leader songs:
- Hey, hey, look at me
- *Little Sally Saucer*
- *Lots of rosy apples*

Pitch songs:
- *Chest, chest, knee, toe*
- Rain on the green grass

HOT SONG
- Early in the morning

TOP TIPS
- Pitch cannot be seen – it has to be sensed by the ears
- Reminder: for secure collective song-start, <u>you</u> sing phrase 1 <u>before</u> children join in

TEACHING IDEAS

Set One
'Little Sally Saucer'
- An early opportunity for individuals to have a lead role

'Lots of rosy apples'
- Gives individuals a chance to sing phrases 1 & 2, or phrase 2 only

'Hey, hey, look at me'
- For individuals with growing confidence

Set Two
Pitch awareness:
- You hum a low, long sound with low hand position; class copies
- You hum a high, long sound with high hand position; class copies
- You hum a low sound with hand low; slide sound and hand up to new level, sustain; move to a new higher level, sustain; repeat with class joining in

Sing 'Pitch songs' in Key Songs
- Use actions and hand-levels to show higher and lower sounds

Assessing Activity
'Lots of rosy apples'
- Use the song activity

'Rain on the green grass'
- Class and individuals 'hand-sign' pitch levels

LEARNING OUTCOMES
- Children show growing confidence singing alone
- Children begin to associate 'higher' and 'lower' with singing pitch

WHAT NEXT?
- Revisit Unit 2 for skill practice
- Move to Unit 5

Unit 4

HEY, HEY, LOOK AT ME — TRACK 27

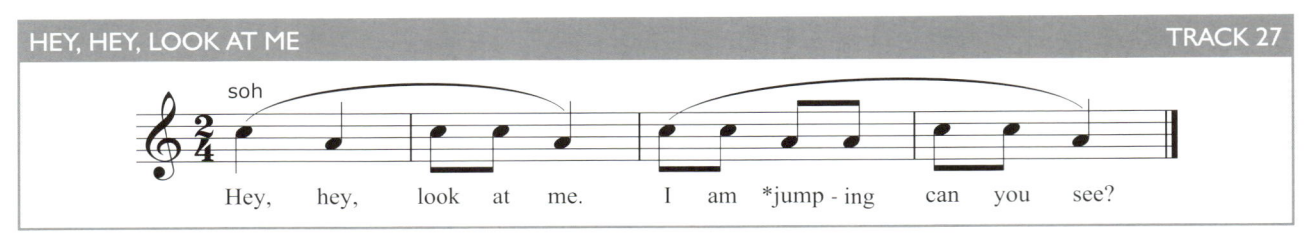

soh

Hey, hey, look at me. I am *jump-ing can you see?

LITTLE SALLY SAUCER — TRACK 39

soh

Lit-tle Sal-ly Sau-cer, Sitt-ing in the wa-ter.

Rise, Sal-ly, Rise, Now wipe your eyes.

(spoken)

Turn to the East, Turn to the West.

Turn to the one that you like best.

LOTS OF ROSY APPLES — TRACK 40

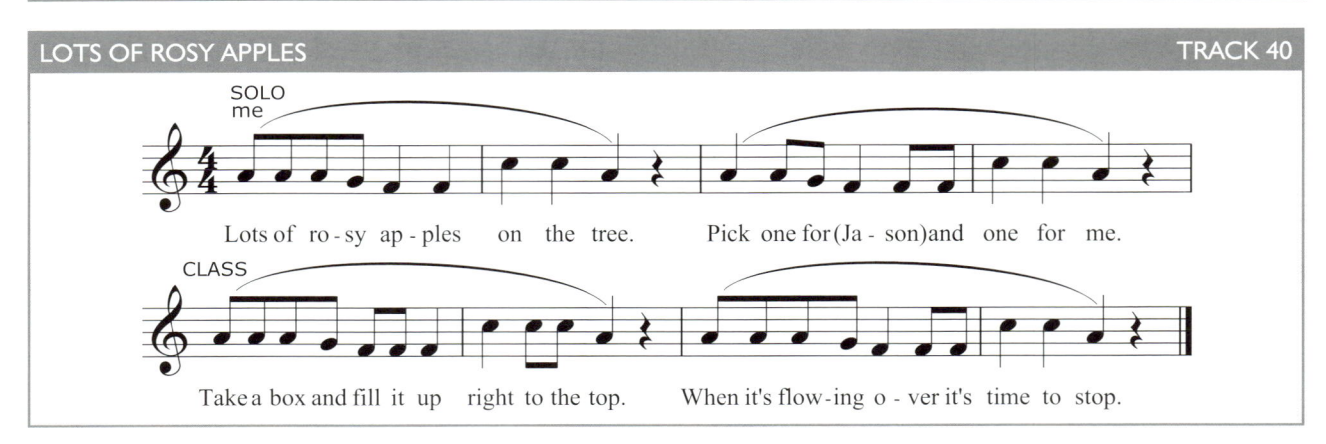

SOLO
me

Lots of ro-sy ap-ples on the tree. Pick one for (Ja-son) and one for me.

CLASS

Take a box and fill it up right to the top. When it's flow-ing o-ver it's time to stop.

Unit 4

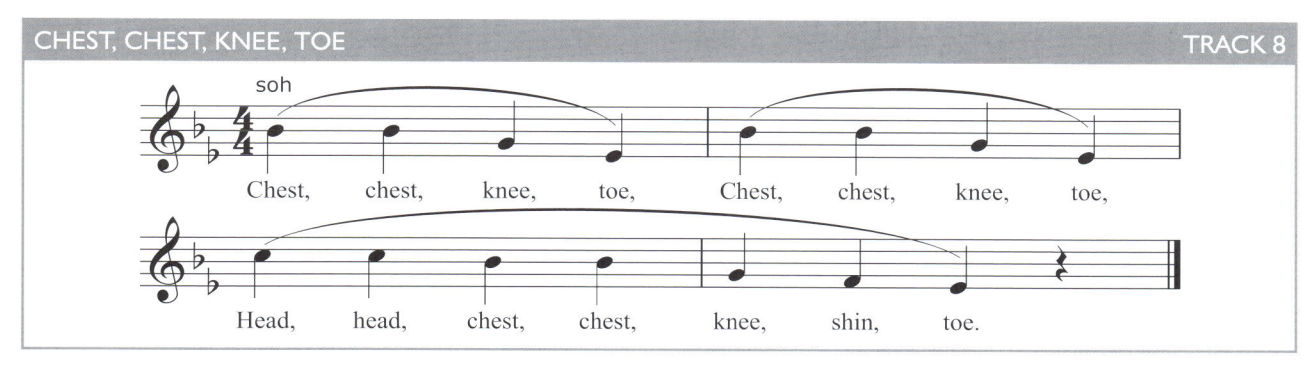

CHEST, CHEST, KNEE, TOE — TRACK 8

soh

Chest, chest, knee, toe, Chest, chest, knee, toe,
Head, head, chest, chest, knee, shin, toe.

RAIN ON THE GREEN GRASS — TRACK 48

soh

Rain on the green grass, Rain on the tree.
Rain on the roof-top, but not on me.

Unit 5

Two weeks

SKILL AND CONCEPT SEQUENCE
- Listening and thinking

TEACHING OBJECTIVES
- To be able to recognise known song melody

WHAT IS GOING TO HAPPEN?
- Song melodies will be hummed
- Children will recognise a song from its hummed melody
- Further opportunities to be a leader

KEY SONGS
Key Songs are known *before* using Teaching Ideas
Italics = first time appearance
- I see you
- Little Sally Saucer
- Lots of rosy apples
- Rain on the green grass
- Tick, tock, see our clock

HOT SONG
- Ickle, ockle

TOP TIPS
- Memory in music is vital
- Each melody has distinctive features that help us to identify it
- Children love games
- Reminder: for secure collective song-start, you sing phrase 1 before children join in

TEACHING IDEAS

Set One
'I see you'
- You and class sing as an echo song
- You hum phrase 1 – class echoes; same for phrase 2

'Rain on the green grass'
- Class sings song
- You then sing phrase 1 but class repeats humming
- Similarly with the other phrases
- Reverse the roles

'Tick, tock, see our clock'
- Class sings phrase 1 and repeats it humming; similarly phrase 2

Set Two
Make list of 3 or 4 well-known songs
- Class sings them through
- You hum unannounced a melody from the list: *"Which song is it?"*
  Class offers the answer by singing with the words
- Hum another melody and a child sings his/her answer
- Child hums song from the list and class/a child sings the answer

'What's my song?'
- You hum unannounced any known song melody; class recognises and immediately takes up the melody with words
- A child can take the lead

Assessing Activity
'I see you'
- You sing phrase 1 – child 1 repeats with humming
- You sing phrase 2 – child 2 hums phrase back

'Spot the Song'
- You hum phrase 1 from the **Key Songs** and a child sings back with song words

Unit 5

LEARNING OUTCOMES
- Class hums a song melody phrase accurately
- Class identifies known song melodies
- Class can recall song melody with confidence

WHAT NEXT?
- Revisit 'Early in the morning'
- Revisit Unit 4 for skill practice
- Move to Unit 6

I SEE YOU — TRACK 33

I see you. I see you.
How do you do? How do you do?

LITTLE SALLY SAUCER — TRACK 39

Little Sally Saucer, Sitting in the water.
Rise, Sally, Rise, Now wipe your eyes.
(spoken) Turn to the East, Turn to the West.
Turn to the one that you like best.

Unit 5

LOTS OF ROSY APPLES — TRACK 40

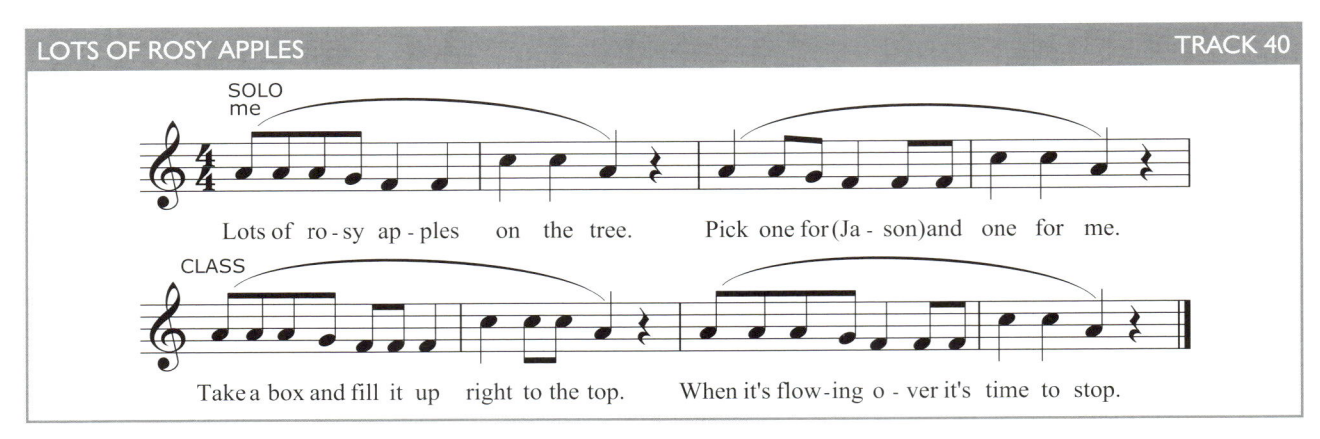

SOLO: Lots of ro-sy ap-ples on the tree. Pick one for (Ja-son) and one for me.

CLASS: Take a box and fill it up right to the top. When it's flow-ing o-ver it's time to stop.

RAIN ON THE GREEN GRASS — TRACK 48

Rain on the green grass, Rain on the tree.

Rain on the roof-top, but not on me.

TICK, TOCK, SEE OUR CLOCK — TRACK 58

Tick, tock, tick, tock, see our clock.

Tick, tock, tick, tock, twelve o' clock.

Unit 6

Two/three weeks

SKILL AND CONCEPT SEQUENCE
- Performing: singing

TEACHING OBJECTIVES
- To repeat a song at different pitch level
- To establish a further routine for a collective song-start
- To repeat a song with changing dynamic levels

WHAT IS GOING TO HAPPEN?
- Starting-pitch for a song is successively changed
- Using *"Off you go!"* for collective starts
- Songs sung with changes of volume [*dynamics*]

KEY SONGS
Key Songs are known <u>before</u> using Teaching Ideas
Italics = first time appearance
- *Bow, wow, wow*
- Early in the morning
- *Engine, engine*
- Ickle, ockle
- I, I, me oh my
- *Rain, rain, go away*

HOT SONG
- Down came Andrew

TOP TIPS
- Quality singing? Stand/chair posture = marionettes with head string taut, but NOT tight
- *"Off you go!"* is sung rhythmically to the starting-pitch of the song

TEACHING IDEAS

Set One
'I, I, me oh my'
- You sing through and class copies
- You sing at higher or lower starting-pitch and class copies
- Similarly, 'Here I come': class sings responses

'Ickle, ockle'
- You sing phrase 1 then *"Off you go!"* on the starting-pitch; class sings the song

Set Two
'Engine, engine'
- You sing phrase 1 and *"Off you go!"*; class echoes *"Off you go!"*; a child repeats *"Off you go!"*; everyone sings the song!
- Process repeated with a pitch change

'Early in the morning'
- You sing phrase 1 and *"Off you go!"*; class sings the song
- You change starting-pitch: sing phrase 1 and *"Off you go!"*; class sings song
- Similarly 'Ickle, ockle' and other known songs

Set Three
'Bow, wow, wow'
- *"Be friendly to the dog, singing quietly and gently"* – after you sing phrase 1 and *"Off you go!"* class sings the song
- *"Now the dog knows you, sing with a nice, cheerful, bigger voice"*; class sings after *"Off you go!"*
- Group 1 sings phrases 1 & 2 = quieter voice
- Group 2 sings phrases 3 & 4 = louder voice

'Engine, engine'
- *"The engine is far away – <u>sing</u> quieter"* – after you sing *"Off you go!"* class sings the song
- *"The engine is nearer – sing louder"* class sings
- Four groups: phrase 1 = group A only; phrase 2 = groups A + B; phrase 3 = A + B + C; phrase 4 = all groups *"What happened?"* Record and listen back

Unit 6

Assessing Activity

'Rain, rain, go away'

- You sing phrase 1; class/child sings phrase 2
- Starting-pitch is changed for repeat process; a child can lead
- You sing more quietly or loudly phrase 1; class/child reflects volume in phrase 2; a child can lead

LEARNING OUTCOMES

- Class can sing to a given starting-pitch
- Class can sing at different volume levels

WHAT NEXT?

- Move to Unit 7

BOW, WOW, WOW — TRACK 3

doh

Bow, wow, wow! Whose dog art thou?
Lit - tle Char - lie Chap - lin's dog. Bow, wow, wow!

EARLY IN THE MORNING — TRACK 13

soh

Ear - ly in the mor - ning at eight o' - clock,
you can hear the post - man knock.
Up jumps John to o - pen the door.
One let - ter, two let - ters, three let - ters, four.

Unit 6

ENGINE, ENGINE — TRACK 14

En-gine, en-gine, num-ber nine, Run-ning on the Lon-don line.
If she's pol-ished, how she'll shine, En-gine, en-gine, num-ber nine.

ICKLE, OCKLE — TRACK 34

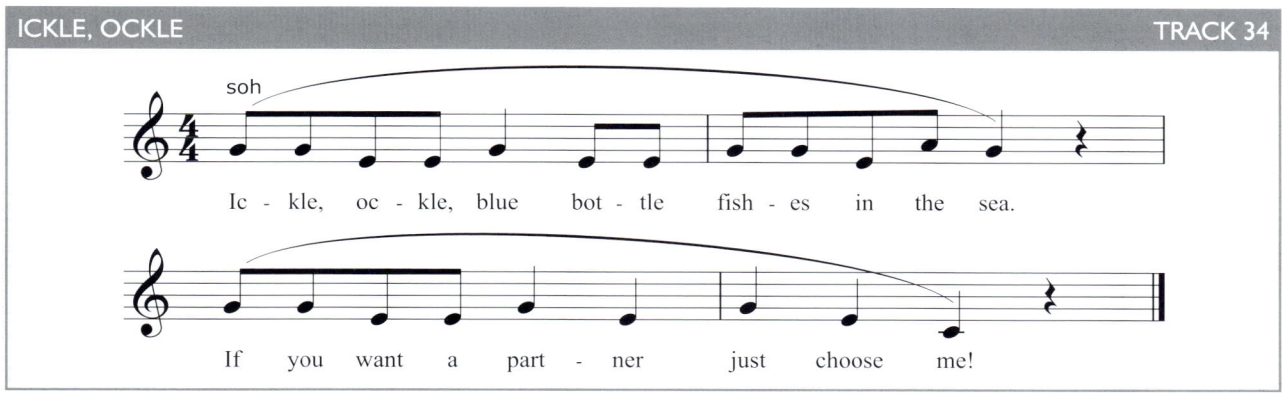

Ic-kle, oc-kle, blue bot-tle fish-es in the sea.
If you want a part-ner just choose me!

I, I, ME OH MY — TRACK 32

I, I, me oh my, how I like my ap-ple pie.

RAIN, RAIN, GO AWAY — TRACK 49

Rain, rain, go a-way, Come a-gain a-no-ther day.

Unit 7

Two weeks

SKILL AND CONCEPT SEQUENCE
- Listening and thinking

TEACHING OBJECTIVES
- To help children to find the Thinking Voice

WHAT IS GOING TO HAPPEN?
- Learning how to use the memory and thinking to 'hear' the inner-singing voice, the Thinking Voice
- Performing songs using the Singing Voice ['real' sound] or the inner-singing voice ['thinking' sound] – Thinking Voice

KEY SONGS
Key Songs are known <u>before</u> using Teaching Ideas
Italics = first time appearance
- Chest, chest, knee, toe
- Doggie, doggie
- Engine, engine
- Have you brought?
- Lots of rosy apples
- *Touch your shoulders*

HOT SONG

TOP TIPS
- ✓ = "Use your Thinking Voice for phrase 1"
- ✗ = "Don't sing for phrase 1"
- Point to head = use Thinking Voice
- Reminder: *"Off you go!"* means <u>class</u> sings, you don't
- See Key Words [page 164] for definition of Pulse [heartbeat]

TEACHING IDEAS

Set One

'Have you brought?'
- Follow the sequence of ideas to be found in The Songs section

'Touch your shoulders'
- You sing with actions
- Repeat with class performing <u>actions only</u> as you sing quietly marking the heartbeat [steady pulse – tap on top of chest]
- *"Sing very quietly inside your head as you do your actions"*
- *"Off you go!"* start: you keep a steady heartbeat as ALL use the Thinking Voice

'Chest, chest, knee, toe'
- Activities as above

Set Two

'Engine, engine'
- You perform: phrase 1 sing ['real' voice] – phrase 2 Thinking Voice [train tunnel] – phrase 3 sing – phrase 4 Thinking Voice
- Class repeats [*"Off you go!"*] – you tap the heartbeat for phrases 1 & 3 [sing], tap head for phrases 2 & 4 [Thinking Voice], all to a steady *pulse*
- Repeat with class also performing the actions

'Lots of rosy apples'
- Activities as above

'Pop-up puppet'
- Choose any song from the list
- Puppet seen, class sings; puppet hidden, class uses Thinking Voice – <u>change only at each new phrase</u>
- Can a child be leader?

Assessing Activity

'Doggie, doggie'
- Class/child <u>sings</u> the question phrases, but uses the <u>Thinking Voice</u> for the answers

Unit 7

LEARNING OUTCOMES
- Children can recall song phrases using their Thinking Voice

WHAT NEXT?
- Revisit Unit 6 for skill practice
- Move to Unit 8

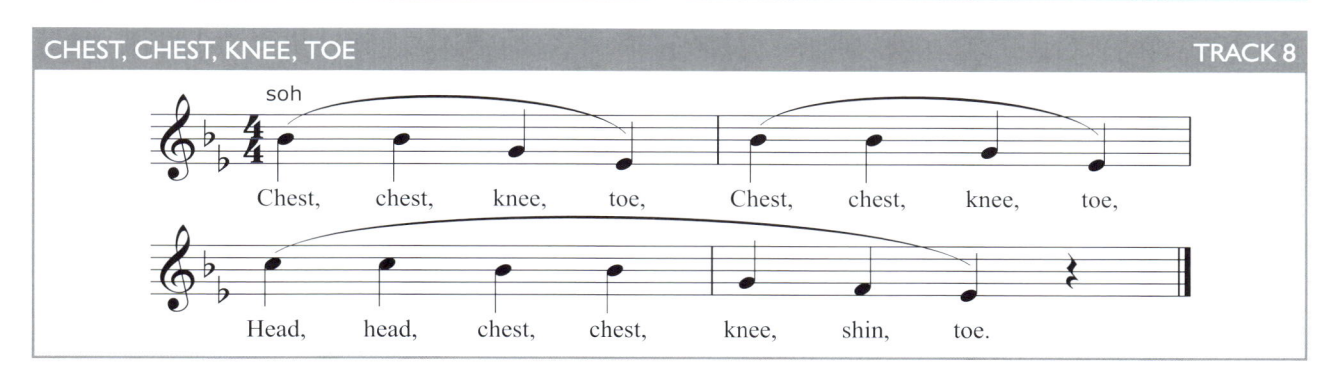

CHEST, CHEST, KNEE, TOE — TRACK 8

Chest, chest, knee, toe, Chest, chest, knee, toe,
Head, head, chest, chest, knee, shin, toe.

DOGGIE, DOGGIE — TRACK 10

CLASS: Dog-gie, dog-gie, where's your bone? CHILD 1: Some-one stole it from my home.
CLASS: Who stole your bone? CHILD 2: I stole your bone.

ENGINE, ENGINE — TRACK 14

En-gine, en-gine, num-ber nine, Run-ning on the Lon-don line.
If she's pol-ished, how she'll shine, En-gine, en-gine, num-ber nine.

Unit 7

HAVE YOU BROUGHT? TRACK 19

CALL: Have you brought your speak-ing voice? RESPONSE: Yes, we have! Yes, we have!

Have you brought your whis-p'ring voice? Yes, we have! Yes, we have!

soh
Have you brought your sing-ing voice? Yes, we have! Yes, we have!

LOTS OF ROSY APPLES TRACK 40

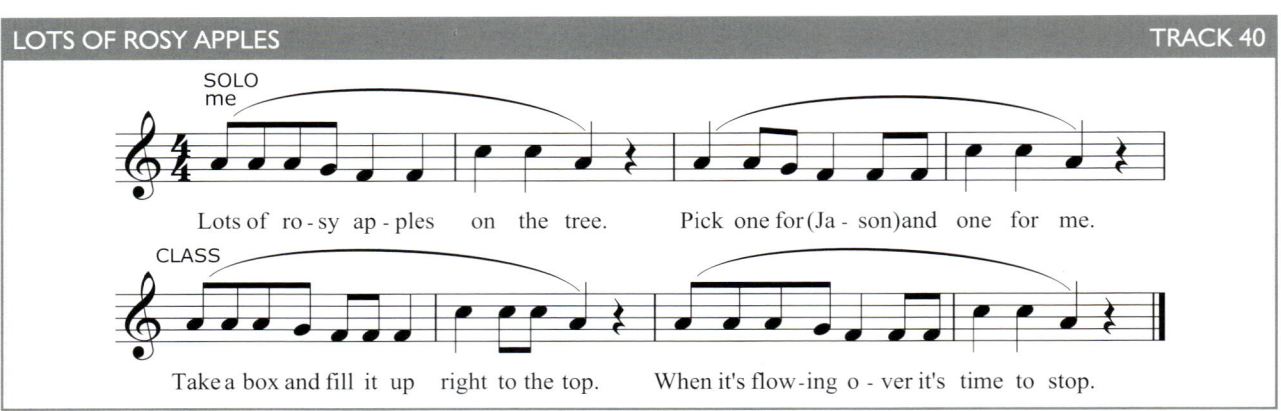

SOLO
me
Lots of ro-sy ap-ples on the tree. Pick one for (Ja-son) and one for me.

CLASS
Take a box and fill it up right to the top. When it's flow-ing o-ver it's time to stop.

TOUCH YOUR SHOULDERS TRACK 59

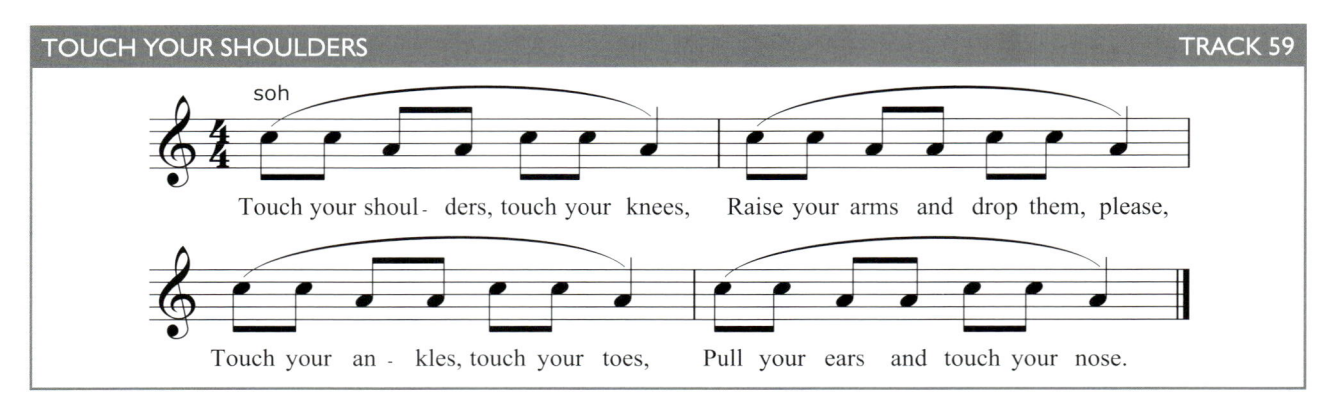

soh
Touch your shoul-ders, touch your knees, Raise your arms and drop them, please,

Touch your an-kles, touch your toes, Pull your ears and touch your nose.

Unit 8

Two weeks

SKILL AND CONCEPT SEQUENCE
- Performing: playing

TEACHING OBJECTIVES
- To be aware of percussion instruments, how to hold and how to play them

WHAT IS GOING TO HAPPEN?
- Hand-held instruments are introduced
- Instruments are held and played
- Care and respect is discussed

KEY SONGS
Key Songs are known <u>before</u> using Teaching Ideas
Italics = first time appearance
- Can you tap your shoulders?
- Hey, hey, look at me
- *Mice, mice*
- Who has the penny?

HOT SONG
- Five little monkeys

TOP TIPS
- When using percussion, think: fewer instruments; shorter time; frequent use; quieter playing!
- Children enjoy using <u>proper</u> names like maracas
- Consider helpful posture and comfort for holding and playing

TEACHING IDEAS

Set One
Percussion
- Find single examples of several different instruments [tapping type], handheld, of suitable weight and size, eg tambour, claves, Indian bells
- You demonstrate each in turn, using instrument's correct name

'Who has the penny?'
- Several children each hold an instrument
- You sing: *"Who has the (eg tambour/claves/Indian bells)?"*
- Class sings: *"[child's name] has the [instrument's name]"*; instrument returned

Set Two
Drumming warm-up
- Class <u>shakes</u> wrists gently; same action tapping knees
- Tapping with right/left hand on knees; tap 4 one knee; tap 4 the other
- You demonstrate, holding an instrument correctly and playing; class imitates with a pretend version – tapping best done with preferred hand

Two of a kind
- You play a tambour; child facing you with another, copies

Set Three
'Can you tap your shoulders?'
- Several known instruments on display
- You sing phrase 1, eg 'Can you tap your tambour?'
- Class responds tapping four steady pulses on their imaginary instruments, then sing phrase 2. You pick an instrument: *"Have I chosen the correct instrument for tambour?"*; class approves or points to the correct one

'Mice, mice'
- *"Which instrument shall we play in our rhyme?"*

Assessing Activity
'Hey, hey, look at me'
- Child sings and plays: *'…I have a tambour [claves/maracas etc], can you see?'*

Unit 8

LEARNING OUTCOMES
- Children know how to hold and play several instruments correctly
- Children know the proper names for each instrument used

WHAT NEXT?
- Move to Unit 9

CAN YOU TAP YOUR SHOULDERS?   TRACK 6

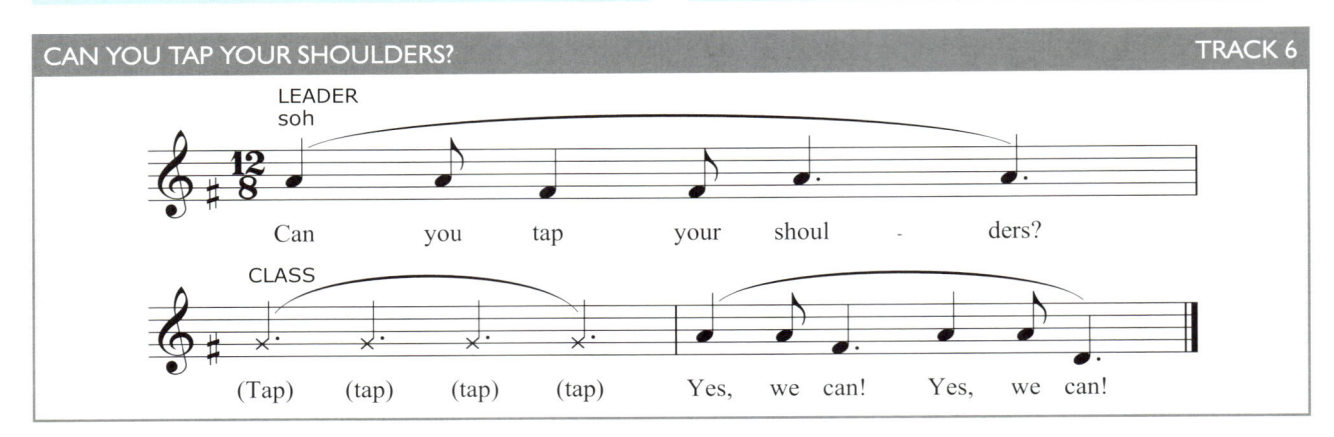

LEADER: Can you tap your shoul-ders?
CLASS: (Tap) (tap) (tap) (tap) Yes, we can! Yes, we can!

HEY, HEY, LOOK AT ME   TRACK 27

Hey, hey, look at me. I am *jump-ing can you see?

MICE, MICE   TRACK 41

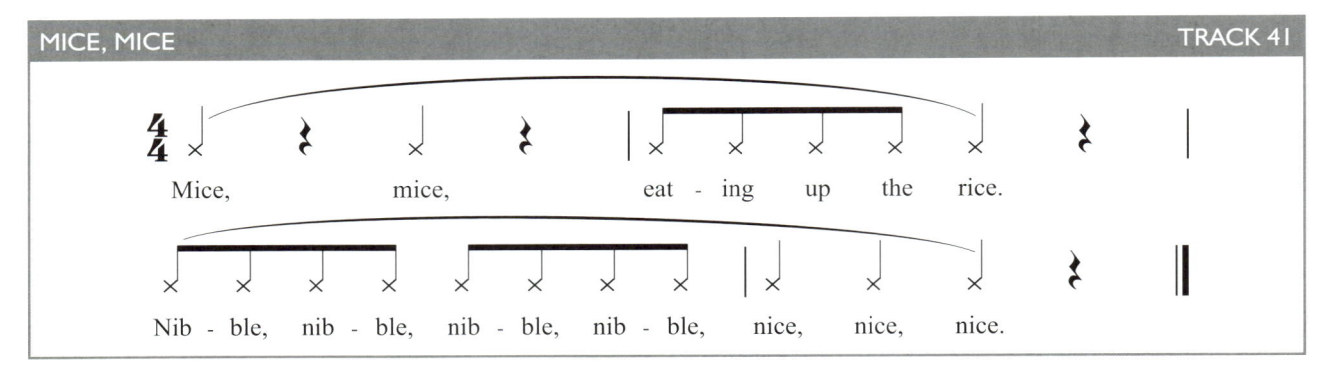

Mice, mice, eat-ing up the rice.
Nib-ble, nib-ble, nib-ble, nib-ble, nice, nice, nice.

WHO HAS THE PENNY?   TRACK 60

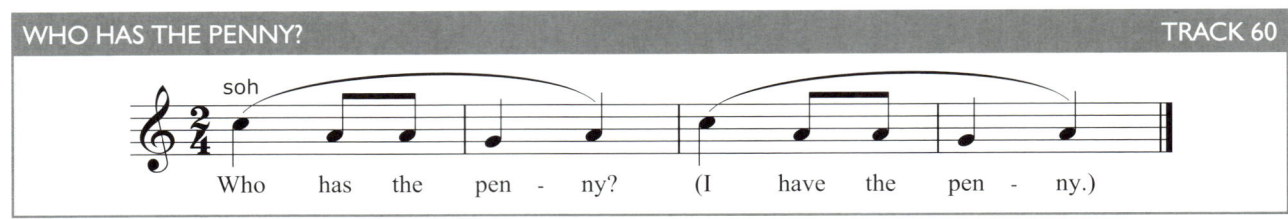

Who has the pen-ny? (I have the pen-ny.)

Unit 9

Two weeks

SKILL AND CONCEPT SEQUENCE
- Concept: timbre

TEACHING OBJECTIVES
- To recognise different voices by sound quality
- To recognise different instruments by sound alone

WHAT IS GOING TO HAPPEN?
- Children are identified by the sound of their voice
- Children recognise other voices, eg adult male
- Instruments are identified by sound only

KEY SONGS
Key Songs are known *before* using Teaching Ideas
Italics = first time appearance
- Doggie, doggie
- *Three little birds*
- Who has the penny?

Key Listening
- Clog Dance

HOT SONG
- Button you must wander

TOP TIPS
- Look for opportunities for individuals to lead

TEACHING IDEAS

Set One

'Doggie, doggie'
- Use the game to be found in The Songs section

'Who has the penny?'
- Play the game to be found in The Songs section

'Three little birds'
- Verse 2: two children out of sight, quietly decide who will say 'Cheep, cheep, cheep', the other 'Yum, yum, yum'; you say the rest; class decides who said what
- Verse 3: as above, but with three children, two speak and the third is 'asleep' *"Who was asleep?"*

Find recordings of voices talking or singing
- Listen and ask appropriate questions, eg male or female? Child or adult? Singing or speaking? One or many?

Set Two

Where have all the instruments gone?
- Three 'known' instruments out of sight: child goes to one and plays it
  "What is the instrument called?" [proper names only]
- Four known instruments out of sight: child plays two consecutively
  "What are the instruments? Which was played first?" [proper names only]
- Four known instruments out of sight: two children play two simultaneously
  "Which two were played?"

'Three little birds'
- Use verse 1
- Three known instruments out of sight
- Two children select one instrument each – one will play a sound for each 'cheep', the other for each 'Yum'; you/class recite(s) all including the 'cheeps' and 'yums'
  "What were the two instruments?"

Unit 9

Set Three

- Listening 'Clog Dance' [Ballet: La fille mal gardée – Hertel/Lanchbery]

Hear Widow Simone's clogs dance: how many times? What happens when the clogs dance? [Everything stops to listen]

Assessing Activity

- Use first Teaching Ideas from *Sets One & Two*

LEARNING OUTCOMES

- Increased awareness of sound differences
- Increased confidence to identify and name the sound

WHAT NEXT?

- Move to Unit 10

DOGGIE, DOGGIE — TRACK 10

CLASS / soh: Dog-gie, dog-gie, where's your bone?
CHILD 1: Some-one stole it from my home.
CLASS: Who stole your bone?
CHILD 2: I stole your bone.

THREE LITTLE BIRDS — TRACK 57

Three little birds all fast asleep,
One little bird said, "Cheep, cheep, cheep"
Down came Mummy with a big fat crumb
And the first little bird said, "Yum, yum, yum"

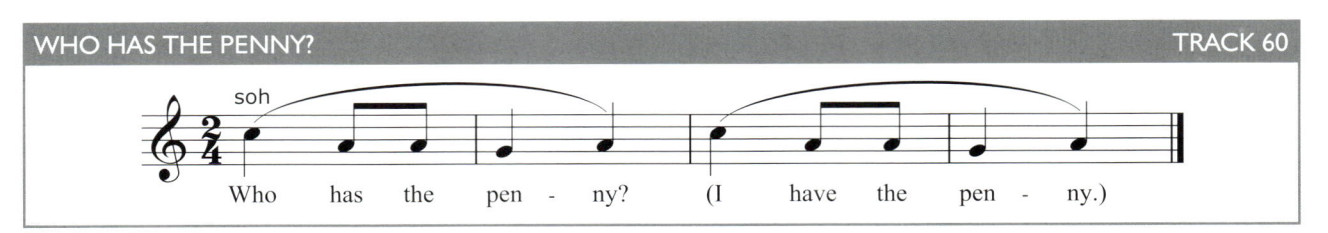

Two little birds both fast asleep,
One little bird said, "Cheep, cheep, cheep"
Down came Mummy with a big fat crumb
And the second little bird said, "Yum, yum, yum"

One little bird still fast asleep,
One little bird said, "Cheep, cheep, cheep"
Down came Mummy with a big fat crumb
And the third little bird said, "Yum, yum, yum"

WHO HAS THE PENNY? — TRACK 60

soh: Who has the pen-ny? (I have the pen-ny.)

Unit 10

Two/three weeks

SKILL AND CONCEPT SEQUENCE
- Performing: singing

TEACHING OBJECTIVES
- To achieve singing with one breath per song phrase
- To develop greater quality of singing sound

WHAT IS GOING TO HAPPEN?
- Children learn when to breathe in songs
- Children discover what is needed to make an improved singing sound

KEY SONGS
Key Songs are known *before* using Teaching Ideas
Italics = first time appearance
- Button you must wander
- *Here is the beehive*
- Ickle, ockle
- I see you
- *Suo gân*

HOT SONG

TOP TIPS
- Children sing best when singing-pitch is higher
- Be aware of poor posture: a slouch is like a balloon with no air!
- Avoid asking for a 'deep breath', it is rarely needed and can result in muscle tension and poor breathing

TEACHING IDEAS

Set One

Blowing bubbles!
- Children blow through hole created by thumb and first finger continuously to your slow-ish count of 1-2-3-4
- Count 1 to 4 with several repeats, class breathes just before each '1'

'Suo gân'
- Class sings and takes an *easy* breath before each 'Suo gân' word [each new phrase]; you support this with arm arc movement like a rainbow, moving across the body and 'picking up' breath for each phrase from open hand on other side [pot of air]
- Class repeats the song, this time, adding the rainbow arc movement

'Here is the beehive'

Sing with above activity - see the song for phrase marks

'Button you must wander'

Sing with the above activity

Unit 10

Set Two

Warm-up to quality singing

Standing tall like a string puppet with head string, but others [hands, knees, feet] loose; a 'pleasure-surprise-look' face; bright star-like eyes; low shoulders; long neck

'I see you'

- You hum phrase 1, class echoes; same for phrase 2
- Repeat slowly, smoothly and with lots of 'bee-buzz' hum to develop resonance
- Two children sing: child 1 uses 'best voice,' child 2 mirrors the 'best voice'

'Suo gân'

- Class hums quietly and gently [lullaby]
- Class sings melody to open-throated 'ah'
- Two groups sing [words] alternate phrases with 'best' voices
- Record and listen

'Button you must wander'

- Class sings and shows the rainbow arc movement for each phrase
  "Your singing should be as smooth as the rainbow" — sustained/*legato* style

Assessing Activity

'Ickle, ockle'

Class/pairs/child sing(s) each phrase with a rainbow arc

LEARNING OUTCOMES

- 'Breathing-with-the-phrase' gives shape to the collective singing effort
- Tonal quality begins to improve for performer and listener

WHAT NEXT?

- Revisit Unit 7 as prep for Unit 11
- Move to Unit 11

BUTTON YOU MUST WANDER — TRACK 4

But-ton you must wan-der, wan-der, wan-der,
But-ton you must wan-der ev-'ry-where.
Bright eyes will find you, Sharp eyes will find you,
But-ton you must wan-der ev-'ry-where.

Unit 10

HERE IS THE BEEHIVE
TRACK 24

Here is the bee-hive, Where are the bees? Hid-den a-way where no-bo-dy sees;
Soon they come creep-ing out of the hive, One, two, three, four, five.

ICKLE, OCKLE
TRACK 34

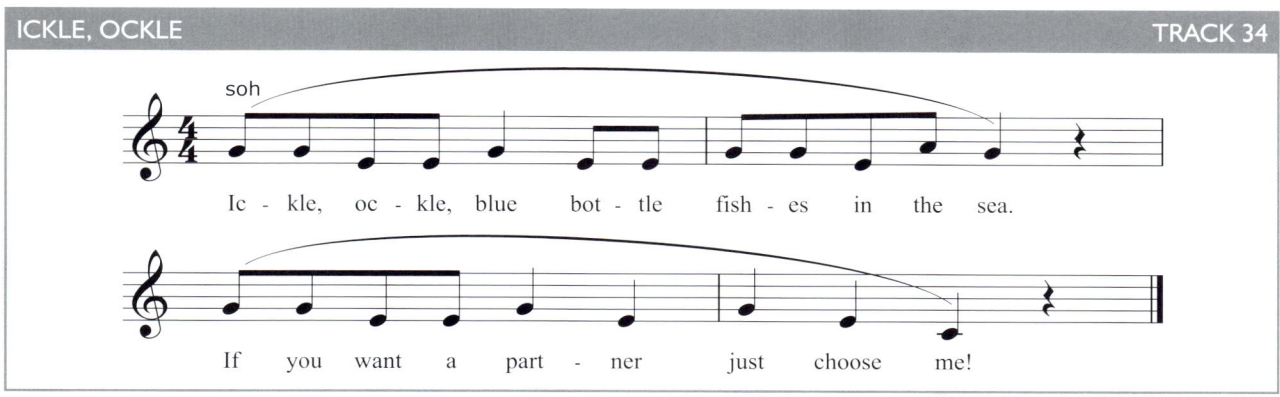

Ic-kle, oc-kle, blue bot-tle fish-es in the sea.
If you want a part-ner just choose me!

I SEE YOU
TRACK 33

I see you. I see you.
How do you do? How do you do?

SUO GÂN
TRACK 55

Su-o gân, do not weep. Su-o gân, go to sleep.
Su-o gân, have no fear. Su-o gân, Mo-ther's near.

Unit 11

Two weeks

SKILL AND CONCEPT SEQUENCE
- Listening and thinking

TEACHING OBJECTIVES
- To develop the aural memory for known song melody

WHAT IS GOING TO HAPPEN?
- Class listens, recognises and identifies known songs from melodic phrases [no words]
- Class uses Thinking Voices to recall known song melody

KEY SONGS
Key Songs are known *before* using Teaching Ideas
Italics = first time appearance
- See Song Suggestions [SS] against Teaching Ideas

HOT SONG
- Glowing candlelight

TOP TIPS
- When children are performing use gesture to signal intentions, eg beckoning hand movement = *"Your turn"*; gestures to say *"Sing quietly"*, *"And stop"*

TEACHING IDEAS

Set One
Song Bag

- Together recall song titles from class 'Song Bag' and sing examples
- You sing to 'nah' an <u>unannounced</u> song melody, class names the song
  [SS 'Rain on the green grass']
- You sing to 'nah' phrase 1 only of unannounced song melody, class repeats with words
  [SS 'Engine, engine']
- You sing to 'nah' phrase 1 only of unannounced melody, class sings to 'nah' from phrase 2 onwards
  [SS 'Button you must wander']

Set Two
Thinking Voice Singing

- You sing to 'nah' phrase 1 only of a melody; class uses Thinking Voices to 'think-sing' the rest of song as you perform a quiet heartbeat pulse; song is named and sung to words
  [SS 'Chest, chest, knee, toe']
- You sing to 'nah' phrase 1 only of a melody; class performs the rest of the song: when you tap your head [heartbeat pulse], class uses Thinking Voices; when you tap your lips, class sings to 'nah'
- NB you make a change just before start of a new phrase; song is named and sung to words
  [SS 'Here is the beehive']
- You sing to 'nah' only part of phrase 1; class takes up singing ['nah'] for rest of phrase 1 and onwards
  [SS 'Lots of rosy apples']

Assessing Activity
- Use Teaching Ideas above for individuals to lead or respond to – *Set One* Teaching Ideas will be more suitable for most

LEARNING OUTCOMES
- There is increasingly secure memory recall
- There is increasingly secure internalising ability [Thinking Voice]

WHAT NEXT?
- Move to Unit 12

Unit 11

RAIN ON THE GREEN GRASS — TRACK 48

soh

Rain on the green grass, Rain on the tree.
Rain on the roof-top, but not on me.

ENGINE, ENGINE — TRACK 14

soh

En-gine, en-gine, num-ber nine, Run-ning on the Lon-don line.
If she's pol-ished, how she'll shine, En-gine, en-gine, num-ber nine.

BUTTON YOU MUST WANDER — TRACK 4

doh

But-ton you must wan-der, wan-der, wan-der,
But-ton you must wan-der ev-'ry-where.
Bright eyes will find you, Sharp eyes will find you,
But-ton you must wan-der ev-'ry-where.

Unit 11

CHEST, CHEST, KNEE, TOE — TRACK 8

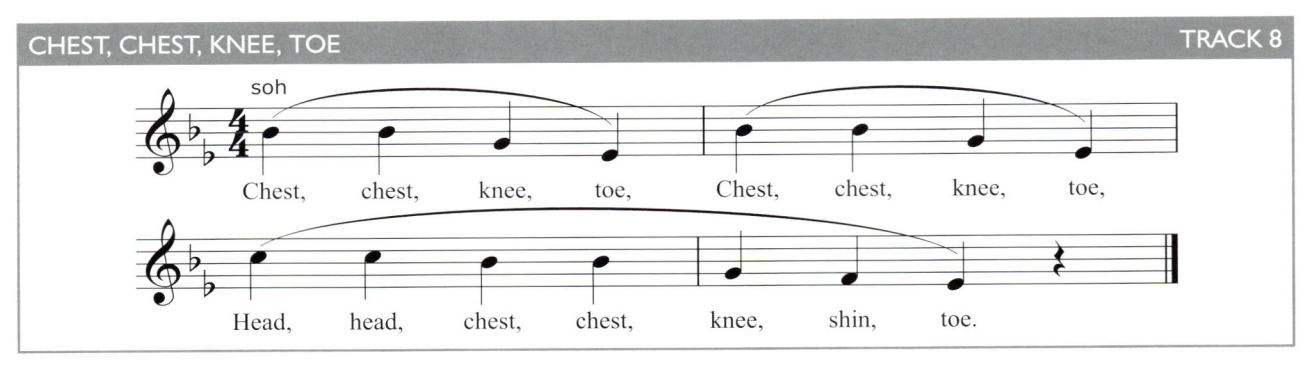

Chest, chest, knee, toe, Chest, chest, knee, toe,
Head, head, chest, chest, knee, shin, toe.

HERE IS THE BEEHIVE — TRACK 24

Here is the bee-hive, Where are the bees? Hid-den a-way where no-bo-dy sees;
Soon they come creep-ing out of the hive, One, two, three, four, five.

LOTS OF ROSY APPLES — TRACK 40

SOLO
Lots of ro-sy ap-ples on the tree. Pick one for (Ja-son) and one for me.

CLASS
Take a box and fill it up right to the top. When it's flow-ing o-ver it's time to stop.

Unit 12

Three/four weeks

SKILL AND CONCEPT SEQUENCE
- Performing: singing and playing

TEACHING OBJECTIVES
- To learn to perform song rhythms
- To perform actions to the feel of pulse
- To learn to play rhythms on percussion

WHAT IS GOING TO HAPPEN?
- Experiencing song rhythms through speaking and tapping
- Feeling the sensation of pulse as songs are performed
- Playing known song rhythms on percussion

KEY SONGS
Key Songs are known <u>before</u> using Teaching Ideas
Italics = first time appearance

Rhythm/pulse
- Copy me
- Suo gân
- Touch your shoulders

Rhythm
- *Can you tap this rhythm?*
- *Here sits a fat cat*
- *On a log*

HOT SONG
- Listen, listen, here I come

TOP TIPS
- Show by 'doing', NOT 'talking about' – it's easier for children
- With 'instrument respect', instruments last longer
- Hand-held percussion: tap with preferred hand

TEACHING IDEAS

Set One
Class sings a song from Key Songs
- You <u>speak</u> its words in tempo [rhythm of the song's melody] one phrase at a time; class repeats
- Work with other Key Song phrases

Set Two
Class sings a song from Key Songs
- You <u>speak</u> its words and tap the 'word pattern' [two fingers onto palm] one phrase at a time; *"Let your fingers say the words"* – class repeats
- Work with other Key Song phrases

Set Three
Class sings a song from Key Songs
- You 'sing' phrase 1 with Thinking Voice and tap the 'word pattern' [the rhythm]
  "Use your Thinking Voice and tapping to 'hear' the words" – class repeats
- Work with other Key Song phrases

Set Four
- Perform songs that ask for a repeated or regular action, eg 'Touch your shoulders', 'Hey, hey, look at me', 'Chest, chest, knee, toe'
- Perform songs adding a heartbeat action, ie gently tapping chest

Set Five
Class sings a song from Key Songs
- Class speaks the words and taps the rhythm phrases
- Class uses Thinking Voices and taps the phrases, you use an instrument
- Use other songs similarly, but several children perform on percussion
- 'Can you tap this rhythm?': you sing phrase 1 only, then tap a Key Song phrase for class to copy

Assessing Activity
You choose 3 song <u>phrases</u>, and class sings and taps the rhythm of each
- You tap on an instrument the rhythm of one unannounced song phrase
  "Which song was performed?"
- Individuals similarly choose one and perform

Unit 12

LEARNING OUTCOMES	WHAT NEXT?
■ Children can perform song rhythm phrases, sometimes using instruments ■ Children know that performing music gives rise to a feeling of regular pulsation [*pulse*]	■ Revisit Unit 10 as prep for Unit 13 ■ Move to Unit 13

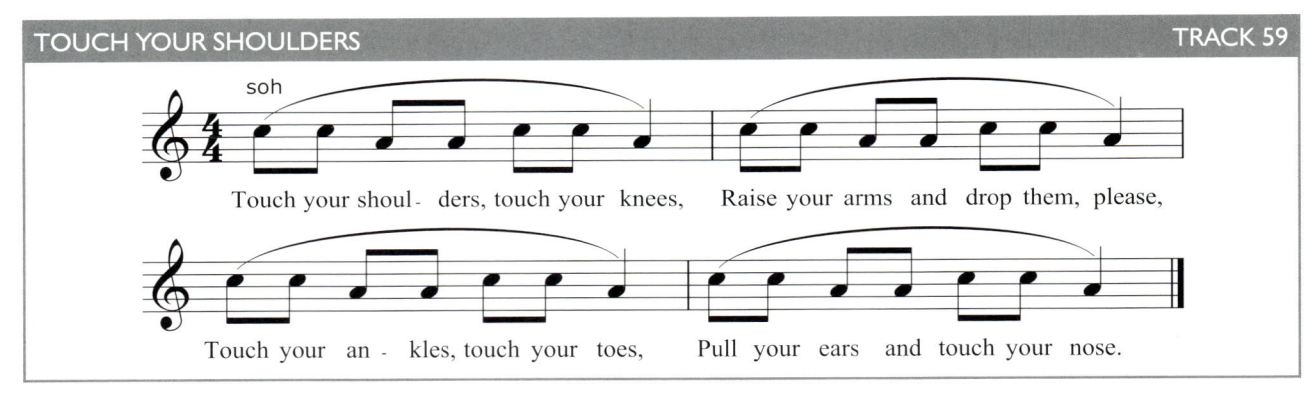

COPY ME — TRACK 9

Co-py me, co-py me, You can do it too! Co-py me, co-py me, Then I'll co-py you.

SUO GÂN — TRACK 55

Su - o gân, do not weep. Su - o gân, go to sleep.
Su - o gân, have no fear. Su - o gân, Mo - ther's near.

TOUCH YOUR SHOULDERS — TRACK 59

Touch your shoul - ders, touch your knees, Raise your arms and drop them, please,
Touch your an - kles, touch your toes, Pull your ears and touch your nose.

Unit 12

CAN YOU TAP THIS RHYTHM? — TRACK 5

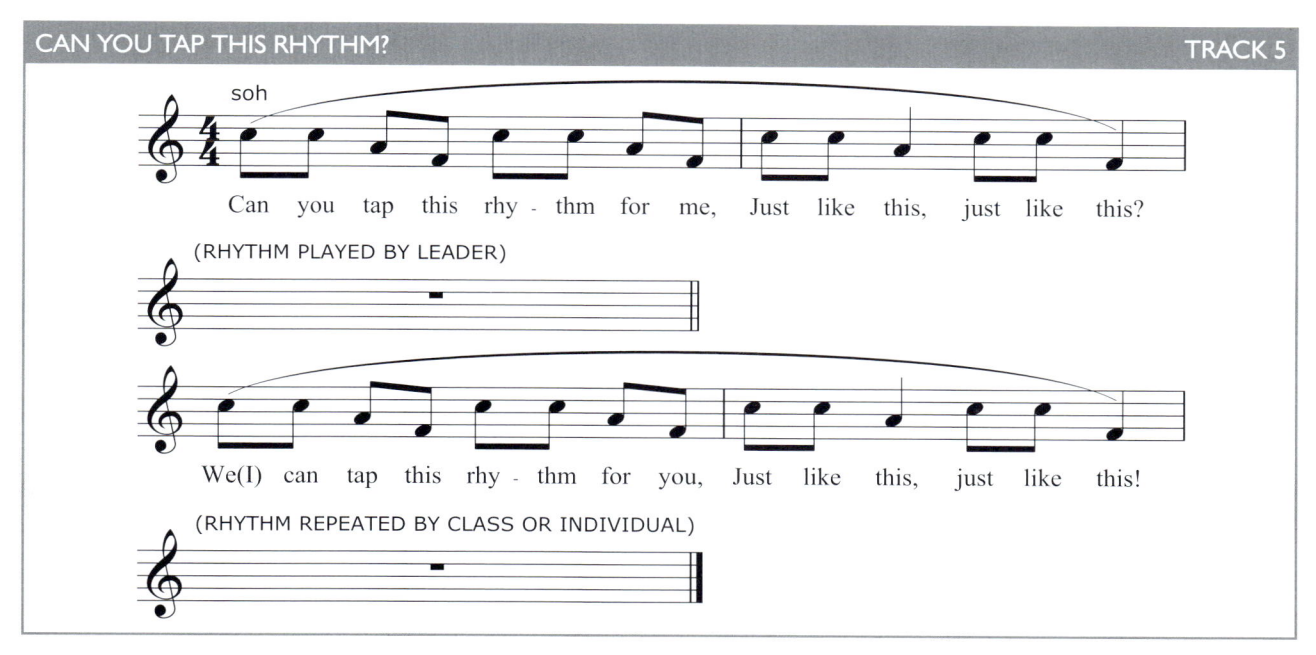

soh
Can you tap this rhy-thm for me, Just like this, just like this?

(RHYTHM PLAYED BY LEADER)

We(I) can tap this rhy-thm for you, Just like this, just like this!

(RHYTHM REPEATED BY CLASS OR INDIVIDUAL)

HERE SITS A FAT CAT — TRACK 25

soh
Here sits a fat cat, Wait-ing for a fat rat.
No - one came to feed her, poor hun-gry fat cat.

ON A LOG — TRACK 43

soh
On a log, Mis-ter Frog, sang his song the whole day long: "Croak, croak, croak, croak!"

Published by The Voices Foundation and Alfred Publishing Co
© The Voices Foundation 2014

Unit 13

Two weeks

SKILL AND CONCEPT SEQUENCE
- Concept: phrase

TEACHING OBJECTIVES
- To recognise the start and finish of phrases
- To identify the length of phrase

WHAT IS GOING TO HAPPEN?
- Melodic phrases are sung by alternating groups
- Actions help to identify the lengths of phrases
- Both melodic and rhythmic phrases are performed

KEY SONGS
Key Songs are known <u>before</u> using Teaching Ideas
Italics = first time appearance
- Engine, engine
- Here is the beehive
- Ickle, ockle
- *Pitter, patter*

HOT SONG
- I have lost the cupboard key

TOP TIPS
- A phrase is a stage on a melodic journey: it sets out, travels and arrives
- The notated songs show the phrase lengths by using phrase marks
- Stand outside the action to help and to assess
- Reminder: class performs, teacher listens; teacher performs, class listens

TEACHING IDEAS

Set One

'Pitter, patter'
- Class sings
- Two groups sing one phrase each, you 'conduct' using hand gesture

'Here is the beehive'
- Class stands as a circle and sings
- Phrase 1: circle faces in one direction and sings
    phrase 2: faces the opposite direction
        phrase 3: faces phrase 1 direction
            phrase 4: faces phrase 2 direction

  You assist changes with an instrument sound at end of each phrase

'Ickle, ockle'
- Class sits as a circle and sings
- Several balls are spaced around the circle; class sings and the balls are passed in one direction for phrase 1; the other direction for phrase 2

Set Two

'Engine, engine'
- Class sings
- Two groups, each sings a phrase alternately; you 'conduct' the groups using hand gesture
- Class sings phrases 1 & 3, uses the Thinking Voice for phrases 2 & 4; you 'conduct' by tapping lips [sing] or tapping head [Thinking Voice]

Sing from Key Songs
- Show a large rainbow picture
- Each child sings and 'draws' a rainbow shape with one arm to represent a phrase mark, one for each phrase of the song's melody
- Repeat, with a child drawing the 'rainbows' for the class

Set Three

Using Key Songs
- Class sings and taps the rhythm of melody
- Class 'sings' with Thinking Voices and taps
- Class sings and taps a new part of body for each new phrase; repeat with Thinking Voices
- As above, but including a new instrument for each new phrase

Unit 13

Assessing Activity

- Two-phrase songs: 'Pitter, patter', 'Ickle, ockle'

  Two children face, one with a ball; ball is passed to opposite child for the new phrase

- Four-phrase songs: 'Here is the beehive', 'Engine, engine'

  Four children face in, one with a ball which is passed to next child for the next phrase

LEARNING OUTCOMES

- Children can 'feel' the length of a phrase and understand that song melodies can have different numbers of phrases

WHAT NEXT?

- Move to Unit 14

ENGINE, ENGINE   TRACK 14

En-gine, en-gine, num-ber nine, Run-ning on the Lon-don line.
If she's pol-ished, how she'll shine, En-gine, en-gine, num-ber nine.

HERE IS THE BEEHIVE   TRACK 24

Here is the bee-hive, Where are the bees? Hid-den a-way where no-bo-dy sees;
Soon they come creep-ing out of the hive, One, two, three, four, five.

Published by The Voices Foundation and Alfred Publishing Co
© The Voices Foundation 2014

Unit 13

ICKLE, OCKLE — TRACK 34

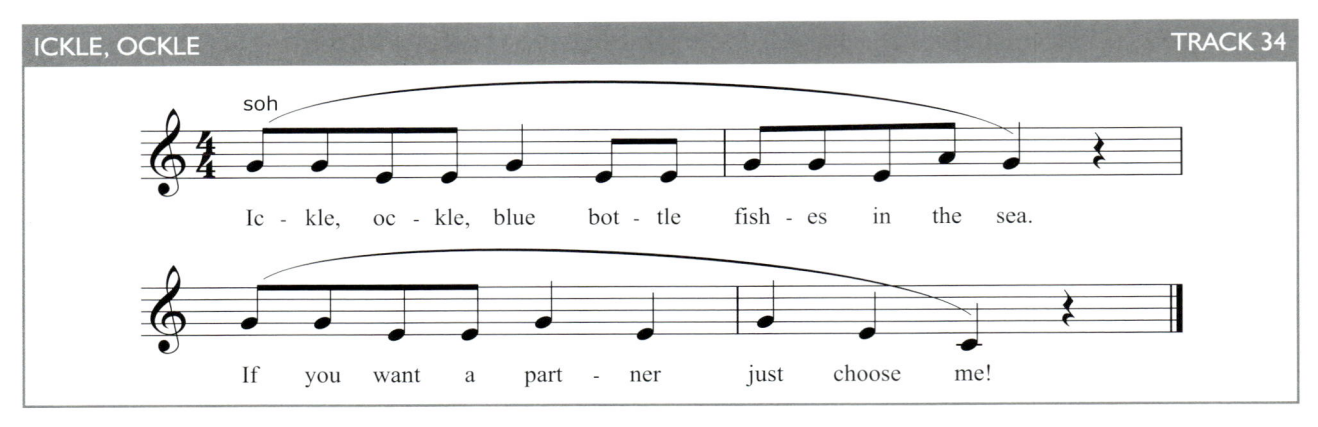

Ickle, ockle, blue bottle fishes in the sea.
If you want a partner just choose me!

PITTER, PATTER — TRACK 46

Pitter patter, pitter patter, Listen to the rain.
Pitter patter, pitter patter, On the window pane.

Unit 14

Two/three weeks

SKILL AND CONCEPT SEQUENCE
- Concepts: dynamics, pitch, tempo

TEACHING OBJECTIVES
- To learn that dynamic levels can be compared as being louder or quieter
- To learn that pitch levels can be compared as being higher or lower
- To learn that tempo speeds can be compared as being faster or slower

WHAT IS GOING TO HAPPEN?
- Songs are performed and music heard to changeable tempo, dynamic and starting-pitch

KEY SONGS
Key Songs are known *before* using Teaching Ideas
Italics = first time appearance

Pitch:
- I see you
- Rain on the green grass

Dynamic:
- *I have lost the cupboard key*
- *Rain is falling down*

Tempo:
- *Peter taps with one hammer*
- *Snail, snail*

Key Listening
- In the Hall of the Mountain King

HOT SONG

TOP TIPS
- Once the activity is familiar and it is appropriate, give individuals the chance to lead: the child gains skill and confidence, the teacher gains insight and information
- Children enjoy using the 'adult' music terms

TEACHING IDEAS

Set One
Pitch change
- You hum low sound with hand low
- Slide the sound and hand up to new level and sustain
- On to a new higher level and sustain
- Repeat with children joining in

Sing Key Songs *Pitch*
- Use hand-levels to show higher or lower

Set Two
Sing Key Songs *Dynamic*
- Sing quietly then louder, also vice-versa
- Compare whispering, shouting, speaking and humming voices
- Dynamic cards: make four cards numbered 1, 2, 3, 4; 1 = quietest, 4 = loudest
- Use cards as the *words* of Key Songs are **spoken** in tempo
- Two groups: A is 'secretly' shown a card to which an agreed song phrase must be sung; B must identify the card number

Set Three
Sing Key Songs *Tempo*
- You sing phrase 1 at 'usual' speed; from phrase 2 class sings and taps in time (pulse) using hand on the chest (heartbeat)
- You start same song again but at a faster tempo; class joins in as before

What did they notice?

Show

♥ ♥ ♥ ♥

(= *heartbeat pulse*)

- You sing 'Snail, snail' and silently tap each heart in turn; class imitates
- 'Rain on the green grass': each child can draw and tap four 'hearts'

Unit 14

Set Four

Listening 'In the Hall of the Mountain King':

- The melody rises and falls in pitch
- The music starts quietly and becomes progressively louder (dynamic)
- Starts at steady pace and increases in speed (tempo)
- At the end, it is very loud and very fast

Assessing Activity

'Rain is falling down'

- You sing phrase 1 to a slow tempo, quiet dynamic and at low starting pitch, the class should continue with these from phrase 2
- Repeat but change the pitch, tempo and dynamic
- Ask class to compare – can they use the musical terms?

LEARNING OUTCOMES

- Children are aware that tempo, pitch and dynamic are changeable in music

WHAT NEXT?

- Revisit Unit 7 as prep for Unit 15
- Move to Unit 15

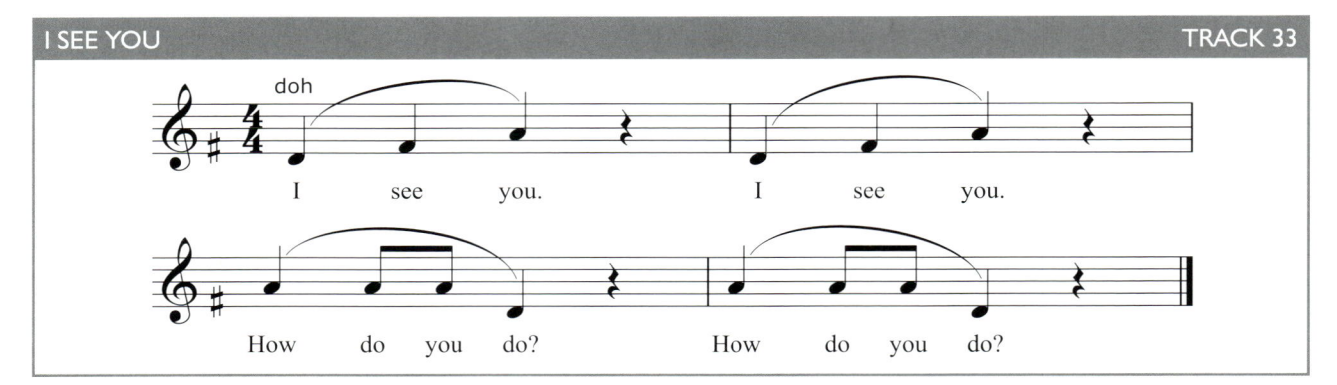

I SEE YOU TRACK 33

I see you. I see you.
How do you do? How do you do?

RAIN ON THE GREEN GRASS TRACK 48

Rain on the green grass, Rain on the tree.
Rain on the roof-top, but not on me.

Published by The Voices Foundation and Alfred Publishing Co
© The Voices Foundation 2014

Unit 14

I HAVE LOST THE CUPBOARD KEY — TRACK 31

SOLO: I have lost the cupboard key somewhere in the classroom.
CLASS: We will help you find the key somewhere in the classroom.

RAIN IS FALLING DOWN — TRACK 47

Rain is falling down. Rain is falling down.
Pitter, patter, pitter, patter, rain is falling down.

PETER TAPS WITH ONE HAMMER — TRACK 45

Peter taps with one hammer, one hammer, one hammer,
Peter taps with one hammer all day long.

SNAIL, SNAIL — TRACK 52

Snail, Snail, Snail, Snail, Goes around and round and round.

Unit 15

Two weeks

SKILL AND CONCEPT SEQUENCE
- Listening and thinking

TEACHING OBJECTIVES
- To 'perform' internally [internalise] phrases from known songs and chants
- To use the Thinking Voice to highlight a particular feature in a melody

WHAT IS GOING TO HAPPEN?
- Children will perform song/rhyme phrases using the Thinking Voice [internalising]
- Children use Singing Voice, Thinking Voice and phrase marks to highlight specific phrases

KEY SONGS
Key Songs are known *before* using Teaching Ideas
Italics = first time appearance
- Doggie, doggie
- *I have a dog*
- Jelly on a plate
- Rain is falling down
- Suo gân

HOT SONG
- A sailor went to sea, sea, sea

TOP TIPS
- When children use Thinking Voices, teacher performs a steady heartbeat to keep unity
- Teaching Ideas repeated over time are reinforcing the skill memory
- A very useful idea is for some children to listen 'in audience' to others, sometimes for pleasure and sometimes to help with the teaching, such as the questions in Set Two

TEACHING IDEAS

Set One
'Doggie, doggie'
- You sing the question phrases, class sings the answer phrases; repeat, but swap roles
- As before but question phrases are sung and answer phrases use the Thinking Voice
- Class sings phrases 1 & 3, but uses Thinking Voice for 2 & 4

'I have a dog'
- Class sings and 'draws' a rainbow phrase mark for each phrase [4]
- Class sings phrases 1 & 3, uses Thinking Voice for 2 & 4 and 'draws' a phrase mark for each one
- Class sings phrases 1 & 4, uses Thinking Voice for 2 & 3, and 'draws' a phrase mark for each

Set Two
'Suo gân'
- Class sings and 'draws' a phrase mark for each of the four phrases
- Class sings the melody to 'nah'
- Repeat, but using the Thinking Voice for phrases 2 & 4
"What did you notice about the singing-voice phrases?" [melody is the same]

'Jelly on a plate'
- Class chants and taps the rhythm on knees
- Repeat, using Thinking Voice and tapping
- Repeat, using Thinking Voice and tapping for phrases 1, 2 & 4, but chant and tap phrase 3 only
"What is special about phrase 3?" [different from others]

Unit 15

Assessing Activity
'Rain is falling down'

- Class sings the four phrases showing rainbow phrase marks
- Four children repeat, singing one phrase each and showing their phrase mark
- Four children sing phrases 1 & 3, use Thinking Voice for 2 & 4
- Class sings phrases 1, 2 & 4 but uses Thinking Voice and rhythm tapping for phrase 3
  "What is special about phrase 3?"
  [different from others]

LEARNING OUTCOMES
- Children are more secure in using the Thinking Voice
- The Thinking Voice is a useful tool for learning about music

WHAT NEXT?
- Revisit Unit 12 as prep for Unit 16
- Move to Unit 16

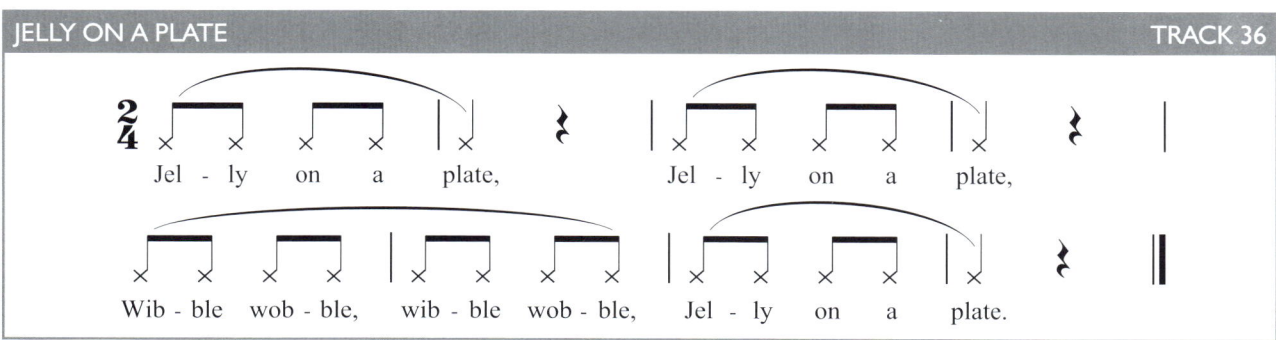

DOGGIE, DOGGIE — TRACK 10

CLASS (soh): Dog-gie, dog-gie, where's your bone?
CHILD 1: Some-one stole it from my home.
CLASS: Who stole your bone?
CHILD 2: I stole your bone.

I HAVE A DOG — TRACK 30

(me) I have a *dog and *his name is *Ro-ver,
*He is the one I love the best.

JELLY ON A PLATE — TRACK 36

Jel-ly on a plate, Jel-ly on a plate,
Wib-ble wob-ble, wib-ble wob-ble, Jel-ly on a plate.

Unit 15

RAIN IS FALLING DOWN
TRACK 47

Rain is fal-ling down. Rain is fal-ling down.
Pit-ter, pat-ter, pit-ter, pat-ter, rain is fal-ling down.

SUO GÂN
TRACK 55

Su-o gân, do not weep. Su-o gân, go to sleep.
Su-o gân, have no fear. Su-o gân, Mo-ther's near.

Unit 16

Two/three weeks

SKILL AND CONCEPT SEQUENCE
- Concept: rhythm

TEACHING OBJECTIVES
- To teach the basic principles of *simple time* rhythm
- To teach and use spoken rhythm names for *simple time*

WHAT IS GOING TO HAPPEN?
- Children perform the pattern of two notes within one pulse
- The performing rhythm names **ta** and **teh-teh** are used
- Song rhythms are performed using **ta** and **teh-teh**

KEY SONGS
Key Songs are known <u>before</u> using Teaching Ideas
Italics = first time appearance
- Here sits a fat cat
- *I, I, me oh my*
- On a log
- Touch your shoulders

HOT SONG
- Here I come

TOP TIPS
- Reminder: *"Off you go!"* is sung to the desired tempo – what speed do you want?
- Repetition aids habit-memory, security and confidence

TEACHING IDEAS

Set One
'I, I, me oh my'
- Class sings song
- You sing it to 'nah', one 'nah' per melodic note – class copies
- Class sings and taps the rhythm, ie one tap to each 'nah'
- Class performs with tapping and Thinking Voice, while you mark a steady heartbeat [the pulse]
- Perform other Key Songs with above ideas

'Touch your shoulders'
- Class stands in a circle
- Class sings while stepping on the spot the tempo of the <u>pulse</u>, you mark the pulse on a tambour
- Repeat, but class sings and taps the <u>rhythm</u>, you perform the rhythm on claves
- All sing, but half mark the <u>pulse</u>, half perform the <u>rhythm</u>
- Two instrument leaders: one marks the pulse [tambour], the other rhythm [claves]
- Perform other Key Songs with the above ideas

Set Two
To a steady <u>pulse</u> marked by your instrument:
- Class speaks the word **tah** and <u>taps once per pulse</u> for four pulses
- Class speaks **teh-teh** and <u>taps twice per pulse</u> for four pulses

To a steady pulse marked by your instrument:
- You speak the rhythm phrase **ta   ta   teh-teh   ta** – class copies
- Try: **teh-teh ta   teh-teh ta** / **teh-teh teh-teh ta   ta** / **ta   teh-teh ta   ta**

Unit 16

Set Three

'I, I, me oh my'

Using phrase 1 only, class:
- Sings song words, repeats to 'nah'
- Taps its rhythm as you tap the heartbeat [the pulse]
- Speaks **ta   ta   teh-teh ta** as you show heartbeat
- Use phrase 2 with the above
  [teh-teh teh-teh teh-teh ta]

'On a log'

As above but with spoken rhythm words for:
- Phrase 1 = **teh-teh ta   teh-teh ta**
- Phrase 2 = **teh-teh teh-teh teh-teh   ta**
- Phrase 3 = **ta   ta   ta   ta**

'Touch your shoulders'

As above, but spoken rhythm for each phrase:
teh-teh teh-teh teh-teh   ta

Assessing Activity

Two for One
- On an instrument you play one sound per pulse, and class with eyes closed hears and taps the same
- You change to two equal-length sounds per pulse, and class hears change and taps the same

From the Key Song list
- You perform one phrase on instrument; class taps back and speaks its rhythm names
  "Can you find the song and the song's words?"
- Above activities could be child-led

LEARNING OUTCOMES
- Children can perform song rhythms and use spoken rhythm names

WHAT NEXT?
- Revisit Units 4 & 10 as prep for Unit 17
- Move to Unit 17

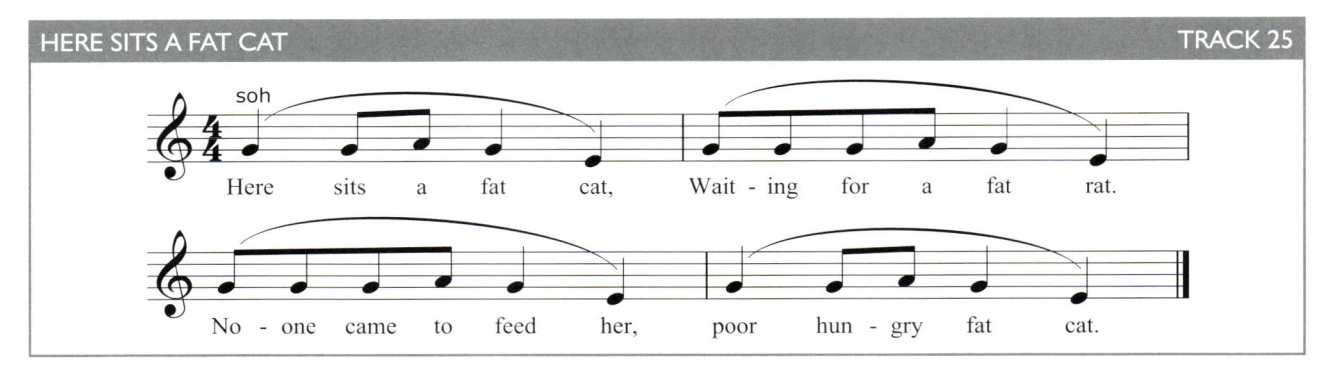

HERE SITS A FAT CAT TRACK 25

Here sits a fat cat, Wait-ing for a fat rat.
No-one came to feed her, poor hun-gry fat cat.

I, I, ME OH MY TRACK 32

I, I, me oh my, how I like my ap-ple pie.

Unit 16

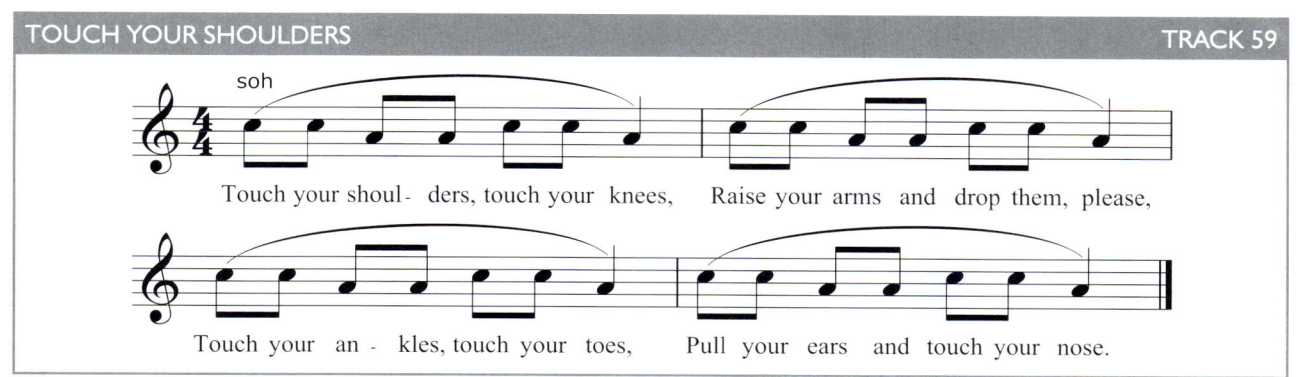

ON A LOG — TRACK 43

soh

On a log, Mis-ter Frog, sang his song the whole day long: "Croak, croak, croak, croak!"

TOUCH YOUR SHOULDERS — TRACK 59

soh

Touch your shoul-ders, touch your knees, Raise your arms and drop them, please,
Touch your an-kles, touch your toes, Pull your ears and touch your nose.

Unit 17

Two/three weeks

SKILL AND CONCEPT SEQUENCE
- Listening and thinking
- Concept: pitch

TEACHING OBJECTIVES
- To listen to pitch changes in a song phrase and to show its melodic line through hand-movement
- To identify and show pitch changes more precisely

WHAT IS GOING TO HAPPEN?
- Children sense the pitch movements in song melodies and show this using hand movements
- Chime bars are used to illustrate pitch changes

KEY SONGS
Key Songs are known <u>before</u> using Teaching Ideas
Italics = first time appearance
- Chest, chest, knee, toe
- Early in the morning
- I, I, me oh my
- *Jack in the box*
- Tick, tock, see our clock
- *Willum he had seven sons*

HOT SONG
- Down came Andrew

TOP TIPS
- Pitch can't be seen, only heard, so aural activity is central; movement and instruments have a supporting role
- Chime bars [the bigger, the better] arranged on a 'staircase' of books give visual support; a tuned-percussion instrument [the bigger, the better] supported vertically can do a similar job – a xylophone is ideal
- When you have illustrated an activity, is it possible for individuals to assume responsibility, eg playing chime bars in Sets *Two* & *Three*?

TEACHING IDEAS

Set One

'Chest, chest, knee, toe'
- Actions and pitch movement of the melody coincide

'Jack in the box'
- Class sings using these hand-movements:
- "Jack in the box … curl" words = hand held higher and still [same higher pitch]
- "down small" = hand moves down two steps [descending pitch]
- "Jack in the box … jump" = hand held lower and still [same lower pitch]
- "up tall" = hand moves up two steps [ascending pitch]

'Early in the morning'
- Class sings using these hand-movements:
- "you can hear the postman knock" = 'knocking fists' descend from higher with two knocks to each of the four pitch levels

Set Two

Sound Signals
- Chime bars C D E G arranged in ascending pitch order on steps of books
- Play pitch-signals game to class: ascending = *'Time to stand up'*; descending = *'Time to sit down'*; repeated pitch = *'Time to sit/stand still'*

'Tick, tock, see our clock'
- Large chime bars/xylophone for notes A, F sharp, D [higher A to lower D]:
- Class sings to starting-pitch A; on reaching "twelve o'clock", all touch head, then shoulder, then knee [pitch descending]
- Repeat; at "twelve o'clock" add note A [head], F sharp [shoulder], D [knee]
- Child could play chimes [12]

Set Three

'Tick, tock, see our clock'
- Large chime bars/xylophone for notes A, F sharp
- To the pulse, play A F# A F#, then class sings; for each "tick" children show a higher hand [eye level]; for each "tock" they show a lower hand [top-chest level]

Unit 17

Assessing Activity

'Willum he had seven sons'

- Class sings the song
- Singing phrase 2 only, ask them to sing with hands rising or falling to show you the melodic shape [pitch changes]; perform with eyes closed?

'I, I, me oh my'

- Class sings the song
- Starting with 'eye-high' then 'throat-low' hands they show you the two pitch levels as they sing; perform with eyes closed?

LEARNING OUTCOMES

- Children are starting to understand the basic concept of pitch, the relationship of pitch levels and how melody has a pitch-shape

WHAT NEXT?

- Move to Unit 18

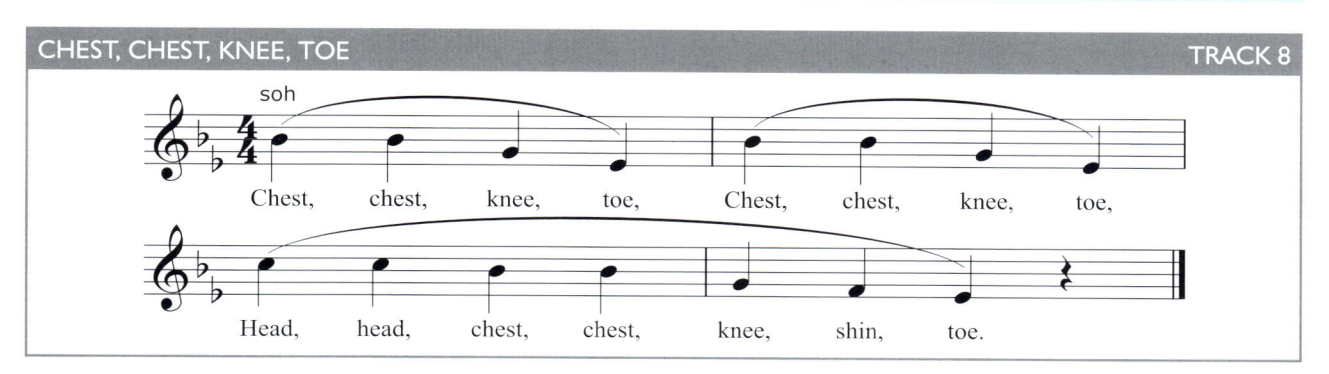

CHEST, CHEST, KNEE, TOE — TRACK 8

Chest, chest, knee, toe, Chest, chest, knee, toe,
Head, head, chest, chest, knee, shin, toe.

EARLY IN THE MORNING — TRACK 13

Early in the morning at eight o'-clock,
you can hear the post-man knock.
Up jumps John to o-pen the door.
One let-ter, two let-ters, three let-ters, four.

Published by The Voices Foundation and Alfred Publishing Co
© The Voices Foundation 2014

Unit 17

I, I, ME OH MY — TRACK 32

soh
I, I, me oh my, how I like my ap-ple pie.

JACK IN THE BOX — TRACK 35

soh
Jack in the box, Jack in the box, Curl down small.
Jack in the box, Jack in the box, Jump up tall.

TICK, TOCK, SEE OUR CLOCK — TRACK 58

soh
Tick, tock, tick, tock, see our clock.
Tick, tock, tick, tock, twelve o' clock.

WILLUM HE HAD SEVEN SONS — TRACK 61

lah
Wil-lum, he had se-ven sons, se-ven sons, se-ven sons,
Wil-lum he had se-ven sons and this is what they did.

Unit 18

Two weeks

SKILL AND CONCEPT SEQUENCE
- Concept: metre

TEACHING OBJECTIVES
- To hear and 'feel' song phrases with a 4-beat rhythm 'drive'

WHAT IS GOING TO HAPPEN?
- Children perform songs and actions with a 4-beat repetitive sequence
- Children perform songs with visual support and instrumental support
- Children listen to music with a 4-beat metre

KEY SONGS
Key Songs are known *before* using Teaching Ideas
Italics = first time appearance
- Early in the morning
- *Down the road*
- Here is the beehive
- *Spinning top*
- Willum he had seven sons

Key Listening
- La Toupie
- Viennese Musical Clock

HOT SONG
- Going on a picnic

TOP TIPS
- Using a known song for the first time in your lesson? You sing phrase 1 before the class joins in, thereafter use *"Off you go!"* on starting-pitch

TEACHING IDEAS

Set One

'Willum he had seven sons'
- Class kneels as a circle and sings tapping the heartbeat [pulse]
- Class sings and taps repetitively the sequence: *floor, knees, shoulders, head*

'Down the road'
- In facing-pairs, class sings and to the pulse repeats the sequence: *clap own hands, tap partner's hands x 3*

'Early in the morning'
- Class sings as a small group walks in a circle, marking the pulse as they step
- Class sings with the sequence: *clap, touch shoulders x 3*

Set Two

'Spinning top'
- Class sings, as one child, to the feel of the pulse, points to the tops in turn, repeating as necessary
- Two groups: one sings, the other chants repetitively '1 2 3 4' as a child points to the tops
- Repeat with two different instruments, one playing at each '1' and the other for each '2, 3, 4'
- Repeat the above, with class performing with Thinking Voice and tapping the rhythm of the song

Set Three

Listening 'La Toupie' [The Top] [Georges Bizet]

Hear the top spinning, slowing down, then being spun again

Listening 'Viennese Musical Clock' [Zoltán Kodály]

Show four clock faces/hearts; child points to each in turn to the pulse of the music as class repeats the sequence: *hands tap chest, silent-hands movement x 3*

Unit 18

Assessing activity

'Here is the beehive'

Class sings with eyes closed and taps to the pulse repetitively:
knees, chest x 3

LEARNING OUTCOMES
- Children will be aware when singing some songs that the pulse [heartbeat] has a recurring 4-beat pattern ie 4-beat metre

WHAT NEXT?
- Move to Unit 19

EARLY IN THE MORNING — TRACK 13

Early in the morning at eight o'-clock,
you can hear the post-man knock.
Up jumps John to o-pen the door.
One let-ter, two let-ters, three let-ters, four.

DOWN THE ROAD — TRACK 12

Down the road, Down the road, Ev-'ry-bo-dy walk to-ge-ther down the road.

Unit 18

HERE IS THE BEEHIVE
TRACK 24

soh

Here is the bee-hive, Where are the bees? Hid-den a-way where no-bo-dy sees;

Soon they come creep-ing out of the hive, One, two, three, four, five.

SPINNING TOP
TRACK 53

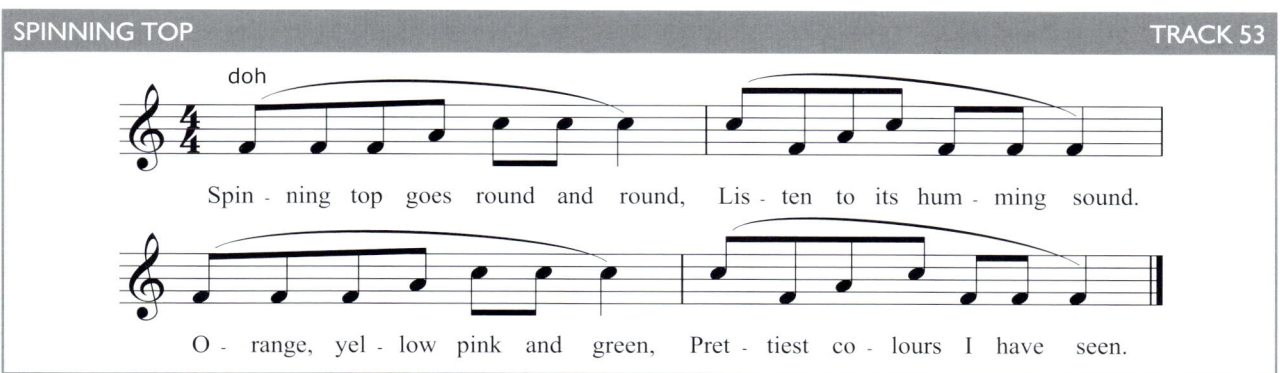

doh

Spin-ning top goes round and round, Lis-ten to its hum-ming sound.

O-range, yel-low pink and green, Pret-tiest co-lours I have seen.

WILLUM HE HAD SEVEN SONS
TRACK 61

lah

Wil-lum, he had se-ven sons, se-ven sons, se-ven sons,

Wil-lum he had se-ven sons and this is what they did.

Unit 19

Two/three weeks

SKILL AND CONCEPT SEQUENCE
- Performing: imitating
- Concept: pitch

TEACHING OBJECTIVES
- To listen to a specific interval [pitch distance] between two levels of pitch in song melodies
- To identify the interval with singing-names [solfa] **soh** for the higher pitch, **me** for the lower pitch
- To learn to associate **soh** and **me** with their supporting handsigns

WHAT IS GOING TO HAPPEN?
- To sing songs that employ the **soh** – **me** interval
- To sing pitch-phrases using **soh** and **me**

KEY SONGS
Key Songs are known <u>before</u> using Teaching Ideas
Italics = first time appearance
- Hello, how are you?
- *Here I come*
- Hey, hey, look at me

HOT SONG
- Here comes Mrs Macaroni

TOP TIPS
- Make sure new songs are known for one week before using with Teaching Ideas
- The handsign 'shapes' and movements support the aural memory and by association they help the aural memory in locating the correct singing-name
- After the class has copied you, allow individuals the chance to repeat your example
- When children need corrective action, demonstrate the 'right way' and let them try again

TEACHING IDEAS

Set One

'Hey, hey, look at me'
- Class sings, using repeated head taps for higher pitch, shoulder taps for lower pitch
- Touching head, you sing 'higher sound', touching shoulder, 'lower sound'; class copies
- You sing **soh** [higher pitch], **me** [lower pitch]; class copies
- As above, but using 'Hello, how are you?': you sing question, class sings answer

'Hey, hey, look at me'
- You sing phrase 1 only, then these 'phrases' for class to copy:
  soh – me – soh / s-m-s-s / s-m-m-s / s-m-s-m

Set Two

'Hey, hey, look at me'
- You sing phrase 1; class copies
- You sing phrase 1 to **s-m-s-s-m**; class copies
- Phrase 2 in same way but with **s-s-m-m-s-s-m**; class copies

'Hello, how are you?'
As above with:
- Phrase 1 : **s-m-s-s-m**
- Phrase 2 : **s-s-m-s-m**

Unit 19

Set Three

Singing-names

soh [mouth level]   **me** [chest-top level]

- You sing 'Here I come' [phrase 1], then **s-m** with handsigns; class copies

- Sing these 'phrases' for class to copy:
  s-m-s-s / **s-m-m-s** / **s-m-s-m**

'Hello, how are you?'

- You sing *question* to words, then with singing-names and handsigns:
  s-m-s-s-m; class copies

- You sing *answer* to words then with singing-names and handsigns:
  s-s-m-s-m; class copies

Set Four

'Here I come'

- You sing as leader, with class singing responses

- Several repeats, but each time you start at a new pitch, the responses must follow your pitch

- Opportunity for individuals to lead in a similar way

- Just using 'Here I come/Where from?' You sing **s-s-m** [+ handsigns]; class respond **s-m** [+ handsigns]; several repeats but starting and responses at a new pitch each time

- You sing and sign **s-s-m-s-m**; then sing *"Off you go!"* and class sings the phrase

- Repeat above several times, but change the *"Off you go!"* pitch which class must match; handsigns are always used with singing-names

Set Five

Melodic Phrases

- You speak the rhythm phrase: **ta ta teh-teh ta** – class copies; then to this rhythm sing the following examples for class to copy:
  s-m-s-s-m / **s-s-m-m-s**

- As above: **teh-teh ta teh-teh ta**
  s-s-m-s-s-m / **s-m-s-s-m-s**

- As above: **teh-teh teh-teh ta ta**
  s-s-s-s-m-m / **s-s-m-m-s-m**

Assessing Activity

- You sing any of the singing-name phrases in *Sets One to Three*, asking class to copy and handsign

- You sing 'I, I, me oh my' phrase 1 with words; class repeats, but with singing-names + handsigns

- Ask child to say: **ta ta teh-teh ta** and to tap, then to sing with added singing-names + handsigns [**soh** starting]

LEARNING OUTCOMES

- Children have embarked on a journey of using singing-names [solfa] to identify specific pitch relationships

WHAT NEXT?

- Revisit Unit 12 as prep for Unit 20
- Move to Unit 20

Unit 19

HELLO, HOW ARE YOU?   TRACK 20

Hel - lo, how are you? Ve - ry well, thank - you.

HERE I COME   TRACK 23

Here I come! Where from? Bris - tol. What's your trade?
Le - mo - nade. Give us some, don't be a - fraid.

HEY, HEY, LOOK AT ME   TRACK 27

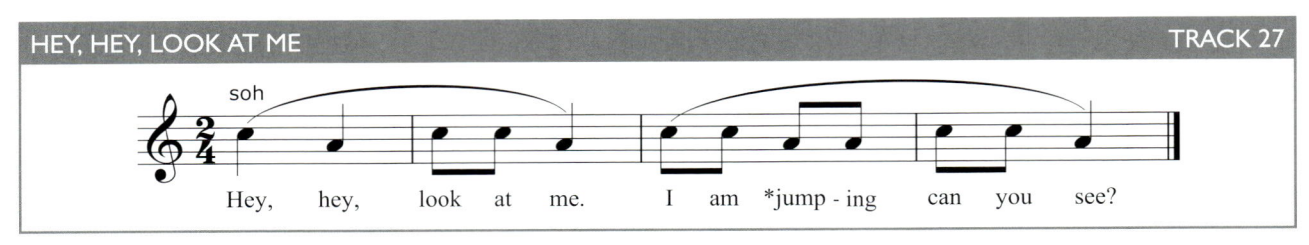

Hey, hey, look at me. I am *jump - ing can you see?

Unit 20

One/two weeks

SKILL AND CONCEPT SEQUENCE
- Concepts: rhythm and pulse

TEACHING OBJECTIVES
- To distinguish between rhythm and pulse
- To feel pulse as a consequence of rhythm

WHAT IS GOING TO HAPPEN?
- As separate activities song rhythms are tapped and the pulse is marked
- Rhythm and pulse are simultaneously tapped and marked

KEY SONGS
Key Songs are known *before* using Teaching Ideas
Italics = first time appearance

- *Listen, listen, here I come*
- Peter taps with one hammer
- Pitter, patter
- Rain, rain, go away
- Willum he had seven sons

HOT SONG
- Follow my leader

TOP TIPS
- Rhythm is <u>performed</u> and <u>always heard</u>
- Pulse is <u>felt as a result of performed rhythm patterns</u> and does not need to be marked and heard
- Give children useful support when and where needed, eg for pulse support play tambour, for rhythm support play claves

TEACHING IDEAS

Set One

'Pitter, patter'
- Class sings and taps rhythm on palm of hand
- Class sings and marks the steady heartbeat pulse on chest
- Two groups sing: one taps the rhythm, other marks the pulse
- Three children: child A sings, B marks the pulse, C taps the rhythm.

'Listen, listen, here I come'
- Class sings and taps rhythm
- Class sings and marks the heartbeat pulse
- Class performs with rhythm, then without pause, repeats marking pulse

Set Two

'Peter taps with one hammer'
- Class sings, tapping the rhythm on palm of one hand
- Class sings, marking the pulse with fist-on-fist taps
- Two groups sing song twice: group 1 taps rhythm, group 2 marks pulse, and on repeat they swap activities
- Facing-pairs: child A marks the pulse, child B taps the rhythm, all sing

'Rain, rain, go away'

Class in a circle:
- Sings and taps rhythm on palm of hand
- All turn to face one way, sing and tap rhythm on shoulders of child in front
- Sings and marks the pulse by walking on the spot
- Facing-pairs: child 1 marks the pulse by walking on the spot, child 2 tapping the rhythm on shoulders of child 1

Unit 20

Set Three

'Willum he had seven sons'

Class:

- Sings and marks the heartbeat pulse
- Sings and taps the rhythm
- Sings phrase 1 and taps the rhythm; for phrase 2 uses Thinking Voice and taps the rhythm
- Uses Thinking Voice and taps the rhythm
- Uses Thinking Voice, taps rhythm and steps the pulse 'on the spot'
- Two contrasting instruments: instrument 1 marks the pulse; 2 performs the rhythm

Assessing Activity

'Listen, listen, here I come'

Class in a circle:

- As the class sings, child with a tambour and <u>soft-headed</u> beater walks inside and close to the circle, marking a steady pulse or performing the rhythm, as agreed beforehand; for rhythm, the other end
- A child walks inside the circle, sings and elects whether to perform the rhythm or mark the pulse – for pulse, the <u>soft-head</u> of the beater is used; for rhythm, the other end
  Did intentions match performance? Did class agree? Does the child need to have a further go to correct the intention? Then you or another child can help by simultaneously using an extra tambour and beater

LEARNING OUTCOMES

- Children understand that rhythm and pulse are mutually related, but are also different

WHAT NEXT?

- Move to Unit 21

LISTEN, LISTEN, HERE I COME TRACK 37

soh
Lis-ten, lis-ten, here I come, Some-one spe-cial gets the drum.

PETER TAPS WITH ONE HAMMER TRACK 45

doh
Pe-ter taps with one ham-mer, one ham-mer, one ham-mer,
Pe-ter taps with one ham-mer all day long.

Unit 20

PITTER, PATTER — TRACK 46

Pit-ter pat-ter, pit-ter pat-ter, Lis-ten to the rain.
Pit-ter pat-ter, pit-ter pat-ter, On the win-dow pane.

RAIN, RAIN, GO AWAY — TRACK 49

Rain, rain, go a-way, Come a-gain a-no-ther day.

WILLUM HE HAD SEVEN SONS — TRACK 61

Wil-lum, he had se-ven sons, se-ven sons, se-ven sons,
Wil-lum he had se-ven sons and this is what they did.

Published by The Voices Foundation and Alfred Publishing Co
© The Voices Foundation 2014

Unit 21

Two/three weeks

SKILL AND CONCEPT SEQUENCE
- Listening and thinking

TEACHING OBJECTIVES
- To listen to recorded vocal music
- To recognise songs from their rhythms only
- To listen to longer pieces of recorded music

WHAT IS GOING TO HAPPEN?
- Listening to recorded music with a focus
- Identifying a known song from its tapped rhythm

KEY SONGS
Key Songs are known *before* using Teaching Ideas
Italics = first time appearance

- Button you must wander
- Ickle, ockle
- Spinning top

Key Listening

- Nun, Gimel, Hei, Shin
- Oliver Cromwell
- Entry of the Gladiators
- The Arrival of the Queen of Sheba

HOT SONG
- Here comes a bluebird

TOP TIPS
- Quality sound reproduction = quality sound reception

TEACHING IDEAS

Set One

Listening 'Nun, Gimel, Hei, Shin'

- A piece celebrating Hanukkah, sung by children in Hebrew
- By marking the heartbeat [pulse], can you and class hear the changes of speed?
- Did they hear the soloist?
- How did the music end?

Listening 'Oliver Cromwell'

- A Suffolk nursery rhyme
- Who is Oliver? What happens to him?
- Mark the pulse – how fast?
- How many voices are singing?
- What other nursery rhymes do the children remember?

Set Two

Key Songs

- Class sings the three songs
- You tap the rhythm, **unannounced**, of a song on an instrument, then to your *"Off you go!"* starting-pitch class sings the 'answer'
- Opportunity for individuals to lead – use of Thinking Voice is vital

Other Key Songs

- You tap the rhythm, unannounced, of a song sung recently for class to identify and sing
- Opportunity for individuals to lead

Unit 21

Set Three

Listening 'Entry of the Gladiators'
- A military march that became a piece of often-used circus music
- Give no title, but ask the class whose arrival in the big tent they feel the music announces [usually clowns!]

Listening 'The Arrival of the Queen of Sheba'
- Give no title, but ask class whose arrival in a large palatial building they feel is being announced by the music

Assessing Activity
- Use evidence from *Set Two* and *Set Three* Teaching Ideas

LEARNING OUTCOMES
- Children can listen to music with interest
- Children can recognise a song from its rhythmic pattern

WHAT NEXT?
- Revisit Units 16 & 18 as prep for Unit 22
- Move to Unit 22

BUTTON YOU MUST WANDER — TRACK 4

But-ton you must wan-der, wan-der, wan-der,
But-ton you must wan-der ev-'ry-where.
Bright eyes will find you, Sharp eyes will find you,
But-ton you must wan-der ev-'ry-where.

Unit 21

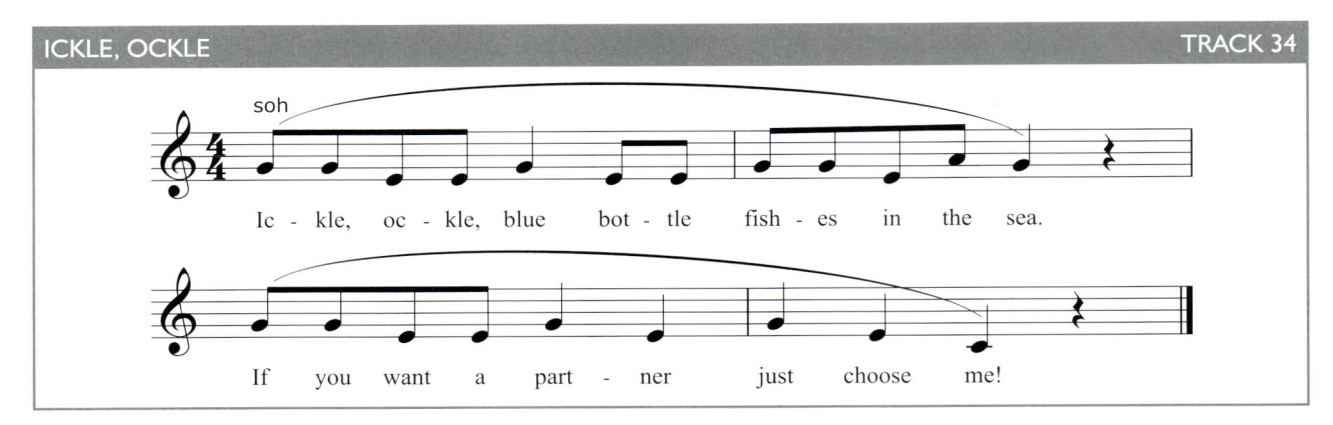

ICKLE, OCKLE
TRACK 34

soh

Ic - kle, oc - kle, blue bot - tle fish - es in the sea.

If you want a part - ner just choose me!

SPINNING TOP
TRACK 53

doh

Spin - ning top goes round and round, Lis - ten to its hum - ming sound.

O - range, yel - low pink and green, Pret - tiest co - lours I have seen.

Unit 22

Two weeks

SKILL AND CONCEPT SEQUENCE
- Performing: improvising

TEACHING OBJECTIVES
- To develop an early stage in the skill of improvising [inventing]

WHAT IS GOING TO HAPPEN?
- Small pool of rhythm phrases from songs is identified
- Known rhythm phrases form the basis of opportunities for choice and spontaneity

KEY SONGS
Key Songs are known <u>before</u> using Teaching Ideas
Italics = first time appearance
- Can you tap/say this rhythm?
- Hello, how are you?
- *Once a man fell in a well*

HOT SONG
- Miss, miss

TOP TIPS
- Ear **before** eye, sound **before** symbol, language **before** writing: practical skills lead to knowledge
- 'A little and often' enables frequent practice of skills without fear of boredom

TEACHING IDEAS

Set One
'Hello, how are you?'
- Class sings marking the heartbeat [pulse]
- Class taps phrase 1, then says
     ta ta teh-teh ta while marking pulse
- Class taps phrase 2, then says
     teh-teh ta ta ta while marking pulse

'Once a man fell in a well'
- Class sings marking the heartbeat [pulse]
- Class taps phrase 1, then says
  teh-teh teh-teh teh-teh ta while marking pulse
- Class taps phrase 2, then says
  teh-teh teh-teh ta ta while marking pulse

Set Two
Rhythm Skills
- Select from *Set One* phrases with spoken rhythm words; you speak, class copies
- Repeat, but class <u>taps</u> in response
- Repeat, but you <u>tap</u> and class taps in response
- Repeat, but you <u>tap</u> and class <u>speaks</u> rhythm names

Unit 22

Set Three

'Can you tap/say this rhythm?'

Using the 4-beat phrases from *Set One*:

- You <u>tap</u>, class copies – use others
- You <u>speak</u> a phrase, class copies – use others
- You <u>speak</u>, class taps
- You <u>tap</u>, class <u>speaks</u>
- An opportunity for individuals to lead

Rhythm Pieces 1

- Display a list of the *Set One* spoken rhythm phrases
- Select one as a 'refrain' and rehearse [spoken]
- Two individuals silently select a 'verse' phrase from the others
- To a steady pulse marked by you, class speaks the 'refrain'; child 1 speaks a 'verse', class repeats 'refrain', child 2 speaks a 'verse', class repeats the 'refrain' again [*double-decker roll!*]

Rhythm Pieces 2

- As before, but the display-list is no longer seen
- As before, but the rhythms are tapped with the help of the Thinking Voice

Assessing Activity

- You <u>tap</u> a phrase, class <u>speaks</u> back using rhythm names
- You <u>speak</u> a phrase, then a child <u>speaks</u> a different phrase
- You <u>tap</u> a phrase, then a child <u>taps</u> a different phrase

LEARNING OUTCOMES

- Children can select from a pool of 4-beat rhythm phrases
- Children are beginning to select 4-beat rhythm phrases spontaneously

WHAT NEXT?

- Revisit Unit 13 as prep for Unit 23
- Move to Unit 23

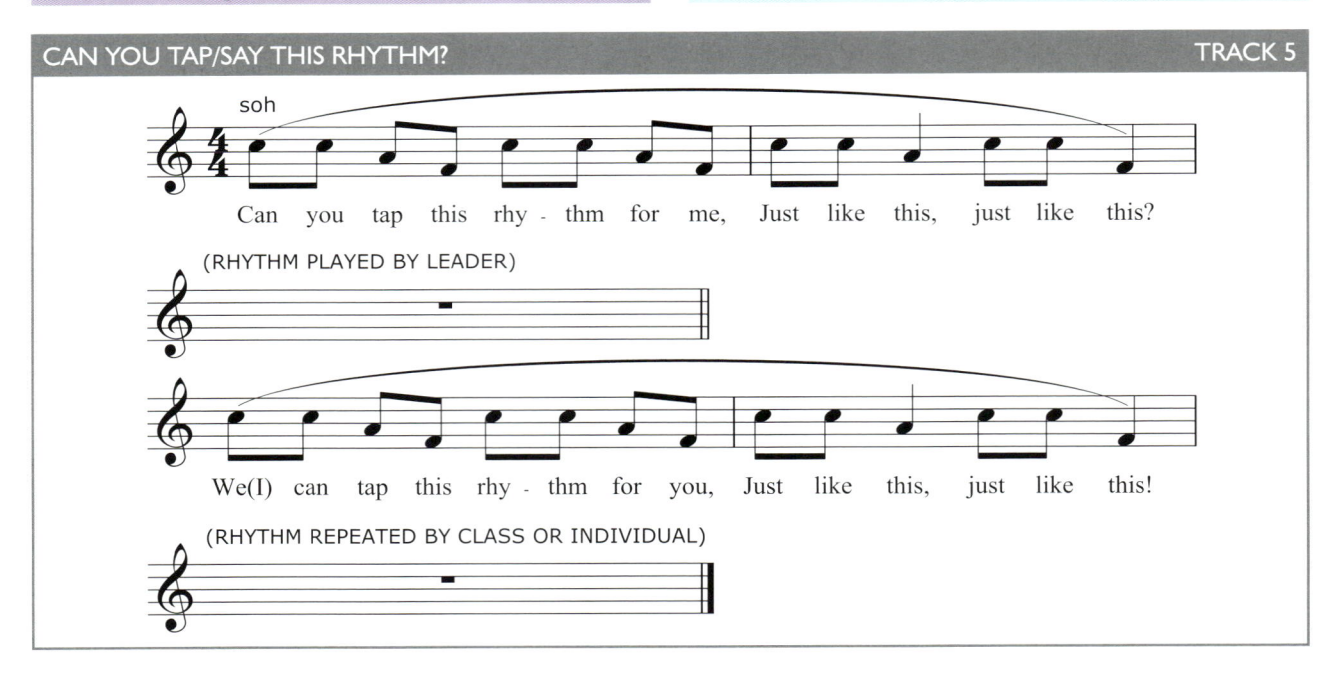

CAN YOU TAP/SAY THIS RHYTHM? TRACK 5

soh
Can you tap this rhy-thm for me, Just like this, just like this?

(RHYTHM PLAYED BY LEADER)

We(I) can tap this rhy-thm for you, Just like this, just like this!

(RHYTHM REPEATED BY CLASS OR INDIVIDUAL)

Unit 22

HELLO, HOW ARE YOU?   TRACK 20

Hel - lo, how are you? Ve - ry well, thank - you.

ONCE A MAN FELL IN A WELL   TRACK 44

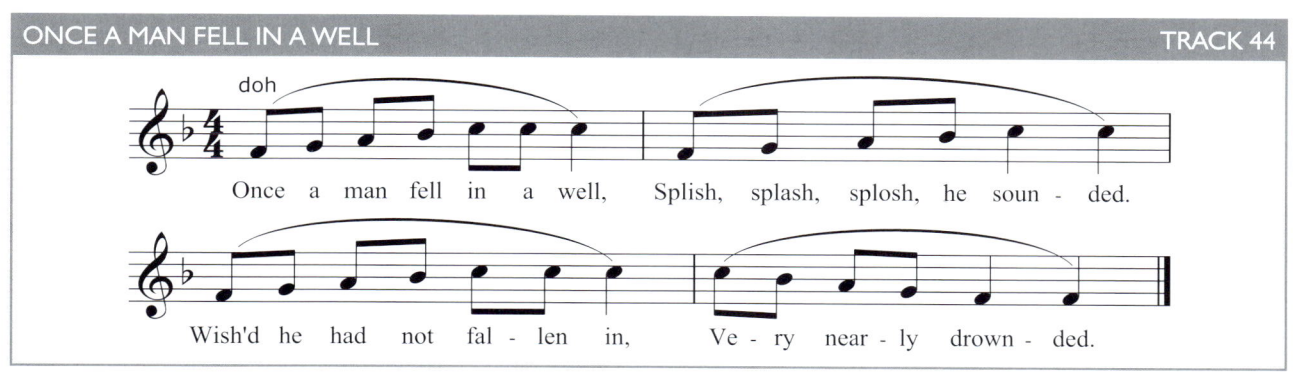

Once a man fell in a well, Splish, splash, splosh, he soun - ded.
Wish'd he had not fal - len in, Ve - ry near - ly drown - ded.

Unit 23

Two weeks

SKILL AND CONCEPT SEQUENCE
- Concept: phrase

TEACHING OBJECTIVES
- To compare melodic or rhythm phrases in a song as being the same or different
- To show that phrases in a song can be of the same or different length

WHAT IS GOING TO HAPPEN?
- Children will identify and compare phrases
- Children will count the beats in phrases and compare them

KEY SONGS
Key Songs are known *before* using Teaching Ideas
Italics = first time appearance
- Down the road
- *Here comes a bluebird*
- Listen, listen, here I come
- Spinning top
- Lots of rosy apples
- *Miss, miss*

HOT SONG
- Round and round the village

TOP TIPS
- Melody has building blocks called phrases; some blocks are repeated, some are different; some blocks are shorter and some are longer
- Pencils can be used as visual representation when comparing melodic phrases: identical pencils, different pencils, pencils of varying length
- Pulse is felt when performing and can be marked by movement; beats are counted and numbered

TEACHING IDEAS

Set One

'Spinning top'

Class sings as two groups, one phrase each
"Is the music of the two phrases the same or different?"
[same]
See 'Top Tips'

'Miss, miss'

As above: same or different phrases? [different]
See 'Top Tips'

Set Two

'Listen, listen, here I come'

Class sings as two groups:
- Compare phrases 1 & 2: same or different? [the pitch or tune of each is different, ie melodically different]
- Two groups use Thinking Voices and tap the rhythm: same or different? [rhythmically the same]
See 'Top Tips'

'Lots of rosy apples'

- Class sings and uses arms to show rainbow phrase marks: same or different? [melodically sound the same]
- Class uses Thinking Voices and taps the rhythm: same or different? [rhythmically different]
See 'Top Tips'

Published by The Voices Foundation and Alfred Publishing Co
© The Voices Foundation 2014

Unit 23

Set Three

'Here comes a bluebird'

- Class sings and taps the heartbeat to mark the pulse, while you tap an instrument

- Each child sings and holds out a hand, palm up, fingers stretched forward; the index finger of preferred hand taps each finger in turn (not thumb), repeating as necessary, to mark the pulse
  How many tapped fingers for phrase 1? [8]
  How many tapped fingers for phrase 2? [8]
  The phrase lengths are the same, ie 8 beats each

'Down the road'

Activities as previous song
Results: phrase 1 = 4 beats, phrase 2 = 4 beats, phrase 3 = 8 beats
The phrase lengths are different

Other Songs

Compare the phrase lengths in 'Listen, listen, here I come' [2 phrases]; 'Chest, chest, knee, toe' [3 phrases]

Assessing Activity

You sing Key Songs from *Set One* and ask children to compare the phrases of the song as same or different

You tap on instrument:

- two 4-beat rhythm phrases, eg

  teh-teh teh-teh ta   ta / teh-teh teh-teh ta   ta
  same or different?

- another example:

  ta   teh-teh ta   ta / ta   ta   teh-teh ta

LEARNING OUTCOMES

- Children become more aware of phrases as part of melodic structure, ie same or different, longer or shorter

WHAT NEXT?

- Move to Unit 24

DOWN THE ROAD — TRACK 12

Down the road, Down the road, Ev-'ry-bo-dy walk to-ge-ther down the road.

HERE COMES A BLUEBIRD — TRACK 21

Here comes a blue-bird through the win-dow, Hey, did-dle dum a day, day, day.

Take a lit-tle part-ner, hop in the gar-den, Hey, did-dle dum a day, day, day.

LISTEN, LISTEN, HERE I COME — TRACK 37

Lis-ten, lis-ten, here I come, Some-one spe-cial gets the drum.

Unit 23

SPINNING TOP — TRACK 53

doh

Spin - ning top goes round and round, Lis - ten to its hum - ming sound.
O - range, yel - low pink and green, Pret - tiest co - lours I have seen.

LOTS OF ROSY APPLES — TRACK 40

SOLO *me*

Lots of ro - sy ap - ples on the tree. Pick one for (Ja - son) and one for me.

CLASS

Take a box and fill it up right to the top. When it's flow - ing o - ver it's time to stop.

MISS, MISS — TRACK 42

soh

Miss, miss, lit - tle miss, miss,
When she miss - es she miss - es like this!

Unit 24

Two weeks

SKILL AND CONCEPT SEQUENCE
- Performing: percussion

TEACHING OBJECTIVES
- To teach skills for achieving different levels of loudness [dynamics]
- To select the appropriate loudness for the music

WHAT IS GOING TO HAPPEN?
- Children practise several skills of playing with varied dynamics
- Children exercise control during changing song dynamics

KEY SONGS
Key Songs are known *before* using Teaching Ideas
Italics = first time appearance
- Copy me
- Hello, how are you?
- I have lost the cupboard key
- Peter taps with one hammer
- Pitter, patter

Key Listening
- Parade

HOT SONG
- Bounce high, bounce low

TOP TIPS
- Height and speed determine loudness: low bounce = quieter; high bounce = louder
- Wrist action: flexible/loose
- 'Skin-head' percussion is more appropriate for this Unit; instrument must be balanced and still, and struck with hand or a beater
- Beware! Children can confuse 'loud singing' with 'loud shouting': standing and singing from the tummy, not from the chest, will help louder singing

TEACHING IDEAS

Set One
Warm-up!
- Class 'shakes out' hands
- Pairs shake hands
- Class waves
- Each child taps two fingers of both hands on knees, in time to your slow-ish drum beat
- With flexible wrists, class makes fingers bounce on the knees [trampoline], little bounces to drum quietly played, gradually bouncing higher to louder [still slow-ish] drum
- Vary your drum dynamic; class responds

Set Two
'Hello, how are you?'
- You sing, and class replies with same dynamic
- You sing louder, class replies quieter; now vice-versa

'Copy me'
- You sing phrase 1, class phrase 2
- Using Thinking Voice, you tap phrase 1 with two fingers into palm of hand at chosen dynamic; class taps phrase 2 in the same way
  The palm is the unmoving drum-head, the tapping fingers are the beater

Published by The Voices Foundation and Alfred Publishing Co
© The Voices Foundation 2014

Unit 24

Set Three

'Peter taps with one hammer'

- Class sings the 'one hammer' verse quietly, 'two hammers' less quietly, 'three hammers' moderately loudly, 'four hammers' loudly
- Using Thinking Voices and two-finger palm-tapping, class performs the rhythm [you play with drum and beater]
- Using Thinking Voice, you tap one of the four levels of loudness, class then identifies which you used; see Unit 14, Set Two, 'Dynamic Cards'

Warm-up to beaters!

Each child has a pencil balanced between thumb and index finger, blunt-end to strike

- Class shakes their wrists gently
- Class gently taps the still palm of 'drum-hand'
- Class taps with greater bounce

'Pitter, patter'

Each verse sees an increase in the downpour, with the singing and tapping and dynamics reflecting this; several children on instruments – last verse: rain has stopped!

Listening 'Parade' [from 'Divertissement' – Jacques Ibert]

The parade is led by a band of instruments
"What does the music tell you about the parade?"

Assessing Activity

- Using the song 'Peter taps with one hammer', individual children perform the rhythm using a tambour; they self-select and unannounced perform to one of the four levels of loudness [see Set Three]
"Which dynamic was used?"
Performer reveals his intention

LEARNING OUTCOMES

- Children have begun to acquire the basic skills of controlling dynamics on percussion

WHAT NEXT?

- Revisit Unit 14 as prep for Unit 25
- Move to Unit 25

COPY ME — TRACK 9

Co-py me, co-py me, You can do it too! Co-py me, co-py me, Then I'll co-py you.

HELLO, HOW ARE YOU? — TRACK 20

Hel-lo, how are you? Ve-ry well, thank-you.

Unit 24

I HAVE LOST THE CUPBOARD KEY — TRACK 31

SOLO: I have lost the cup-board key somewhere in the class-room.

CLASS: We will help you find the key some-where in the class-room.

PETER TAPS WITH ONE HAMMER — TRACK 45

Pe-ter taps with one ham-mer, one ham-mer, one ham-mer,
Pe-ter taps with one ham-mer all day long.

PITTER, PATTER — TRACK 46

Pit-ter pat-ter, pit-ter pat-ter, Lis-ten to the rain.
Pit-ter pat-ter, pit-ter pat-ter, On the win-dow pane.

Unit 25

Two weeks

SKILL AND CONCEPT SEQUENCE
- Concept: tempo

TEACHING OBJECTIVES
- To become aware that speed of the pulse [tempo] is important to music
- To compare the speed of the pulse in songs

WHAT IS GOING TO HAPPEN?
- Children perform songs to various tempos
- Children listen to examples of music with contrasting speeds
- Children decide the most suitable speed for a song

KEY SONGS
Key Songs are known <u>before</u> using Teaching Ideas
Italics = first time appearance
- Down the road
- Engine, engine
- Snail, snail
- Suo gân

Key Listening
- Bydło
- Flight of the Bumble Bee

HOT SONG
- Sally go round the sun

TOP TIPS
- Beware of the rhythm trap! Sometimes children slip into the <u>tapping rhythm</u> of a song when they should be <u>marking the pulse</u>

TEACHING IDEAS

Set One

'Snail, snail'
- Class sings to a slow speed after the tempo is set by four slow heartbeat taps from you, followed by *"Off you go!"* [starting pitch]
- Repeat several times, but you change the tempo of the introductory heartbeat taps to which the song is then sung
  "Which tempo [speed] did the snail prefer?"

'Down the road'
- In a circle, class sings the song
- A child walks the circle with a <u>steady, regular pace</u> and you then sing in time *"Off you go!"*; class sings to the step of the child
- Next child is in a hurry [quicker tempo] – pace has to be regular!
- Next child is tired [slower tempo] NB: The walker needs to move to a regular step, so you may want to support this with instrument taps

Set Two

Listening 'Bydło' ['Pictures at an Exhibition' – Mussorgsky]
- Picture of a heavy, slow-moving ox cart passing by
- Can class mark the pulse with heartbeat taps?

Listening 'Flight of the Bumble Bee' [Opera 'Tsar Saltan' – Rimsky-Korsakov]
- An incident during the opera of a fast-moving, angry bee causing mayhem in the Palace
- Can class mark the pulse with heartbeat taps?

Set Three

'Engine, engine'
- Class sings the song
- Engine travels at 'normal' speed; you tap an introduction of six beats and sing *"Off you go!"*; class sings and taps heartbeats to mark the tempo of the pulse
- Repeat several times, but on each occasion you set a slower tempo, ie train is slowing down

Unit 25

Assessing Activity

'Suo gân'

- Class sings the song
- Individuals sing phrase 1 and class takes up the singing and the tempo from phrase 2
  What does the class feel is the most appropriate tempo for this lullaby?
- Other individuals sing *"Off you go!"* to a tempo that they wish the class to sing to; marking the pulse on an instrument, they accompany the singing
  "Were you happy with the tempo you gave the class?"

LEARNING OUTCOMES

- Children know that tempo is an important feature of musical expression

WHAT NEXT?

- Move to Unit 26

DOWN THE ROAD — TRACK 12

Down the road, Down the road, Ev-'ry-bo-dy walk to-ge-ther down the road.

ENGINE, ENGINE — TRACK 14

En - gine, en - gine, num - ber nine, Run - ning on the Lon - don line.
If she's pol - ished, how she'll shine, En - gine, en - gine, num - ber nine.

SNAIL, SNAIL — TRACK 52

Snail, Snail, Snail, Snail, Goes a - round and round and round.

SUO GÂN — TRACK 55

Su - o gân, do not weep. Su - o gân, go to sleep.
Su - o gân, have no fear. Su - o gân, Mo - ther's near.

Unit 26

Two weeks

SKILL AND CONCEPT SEQUENCE
- Performing: singing

TEACHING OBJECTIVES
- To teach the skill of changing one's own starting pitch

WHAT IS GOING TO HAPPEN?
- Children sing the same song with changed starting-pitch in consecutive performances
- Children compare the starting pitch of consecutive performances of the same song as higher or lower

KEY SONGS
Key Songs are known <u>before</u> using Teaching Ideas
Italics = first time appearance
- Down the road
- Here I come
- *Hickety tickety*
- Rain, rain, go away

HOT SONG
- Charlie over the ocean

TOP TIPS
- Nothing succeeds like success: choose with care the individuals to lead an activity initially – inviting leaders before volunteering hands
- Repetitions of activities on other days ensures success and confidence

TEACHING IDEAS

Set One
'Here I come'
- You lead, class responds
- <u>Unannounced</u> you change starting-pitch for each of two repeats
  What did the children notice?
- Sing twice more, the second time higher or lower than the first
  What do the children think happened?
  Later, this could be an opportunity for individuals to lead

'Rain, rain, go away'
- You sing, class repeats and remembers the pitch; you now sing with a higher or lower starting-pitch ['pitch-cloud'?!], class repeats
  Does the class think the second time pitch is lower or higher than the first?
- You sing the song twice, each time at a different pitch; first time the children put hands on head; the second time they decide whether to put hands high for a higher pitch, or down for a lower pitch
  Later, this could be an opportunity for individuals to lead

Set Two
'Hickety tickety'
- Two children: child 1 sings question, child 2 answers at 'question-pitch'
- Child 2 now sings question at a different pitch, child 1 uses same pitch for answer; class shows with hands up or down whether the second time pitch was higher or lower – the leaders may need to arbitrate!

Assessing Activity
'Down the road'
- Class sings the song
- Two individuals, in succession and at different pitch levels, sing phrase 1 before class joins in
  "Who took the higher 'pitch-road'? Who took the lower 'pitch-road'?"

Unit 26

LEARNING OUTCOMES
- Children have started to acquire the skill of comparing the starting-pitch of consecutive performances of the same song
- Children are beginning to predetermine the starting-pitch of a song using the Thinking Voice and memory

WHAT NEXT?
- Revisit Unit 16 as prep for Unit 27
- Move to Unit 27

DOWN THE ROAD — TRACK 12

me

Down the road, Down the road, Ev-'ry-bo-dy walk to-ge-ther down the road.

HERE I COME — TRACK 23

soh

Here I come! Where from? Bris-tol. What's your trade?

Le-mo-nade. Give us some, don't be a-fraid.

Unit 26

HICKETY TICKETY — TRACK 28

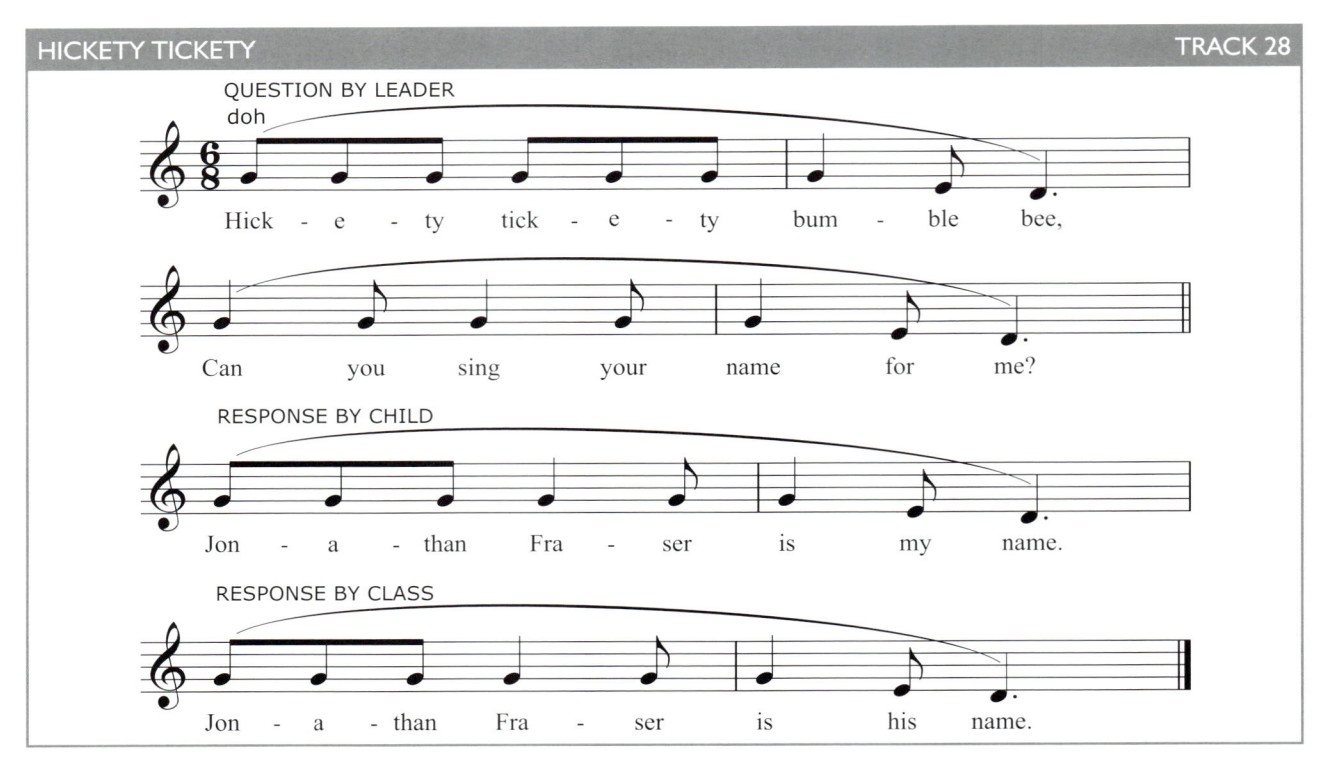

QUESTION BY LEADER
doh
Hick - e - ty tick - e - ty bum - ble bee,
Can you sing your name for me?

RESPONSE BY CHILD
Jon - a - than Fra - ser is my name.

RESPONSE BY CLASS
Jon - a - than Fra - ser is his name.

RAIN, RAIN, GO AWAY — TRACK 49

soh
Rain, rain, go a - way, Come a - gain a - no - ther day.

Unit 27

Two/three weeks

SKILL AND CONCEPT SEQUENCE
- Concepts: rhythm

TEACHING OBJECTIVES
- To introduce and understand Simple Time stick notation using **ta** and **teh-teh**
- To read and write phrases using stick notation

WHAT IS GOING TO HAPPEN?
- Class uses spoken rhythm names: **ta** and **teh-teh**
- Rhythm People are used to show rhythm
- Stick notation is shown, read and drawn
- Individuals begin to select and draw 4-beat phrases

KEY SONGS
Key Songs are known <u>before</u> using Teaching Ideas
Italics = first time appearance
- Here sits a fat cat
- On a log
- Rain, rain, go away

HOT SONG
- There was a man

TOP TIPS
- Always speak rhythm names first before performing or writing a phrase
- Rhythm People: invent games for groups to form up as a 4-'chair' [beat] rhythm
- Rhythm cards: invent card games like 'Snap!'

TEACHING IDEAS

Set One

'Here sits a fat cat'
- Class sings and marks heartbeat
- Class sings and taps rhythm
- Class sing and taps rhythm of phrase 1
- Class 'sings' with Thinking Voice and taps phrase 1
- Class speaks phrase 1 with rhythm names:

      ta   teh-teh   ta   ta

- As before but with phrase 2:

      teh-teh teh-teh   ta   ta

'Here sits a fat cat'
- Rhythm People for phrase 1 [chairs = pulse children = rhythm]

  Position chairs and children thus:

  To a set tempo class reads left to right:

      ta   teh-teh   ta   ta

- Phrase 2 requires 6 people

  [teh-teh teh-teh ta ta]

'Rain, rain, go away'

Rhythm People
- Phrase 1 = **ta ta teh-teh ta** [5 people]
- Phrase 2 = **teh-teh teh-teh teh-teh ta** [7 people]

Unit 27

Set Two

'Rain, rain, go away'

Stick notation

- Show phrase 1:
  To marked heartbeat class says

  | | | ⌐⌐ |
  ta   ta   teh - teh   ta

'On a log'

- Show phrase 1:
  To marked heartbeat class says

  ⌐⌐ | ⌐⌐ |
  teh - teh   ta   teh - teh   ta

'Here sits a fat cat'

- Show phrase 2:
  To marked heartbeat class says

  ⌐⌐ ⌐⌐ | |
  teh - teh   teh - teh   ta   ta

Set Three

Reading cards [on CD]

- Show this reading card:
  To marked heartbeat class says

  | | | |
  ta   ta   ta   ta

- Show a series of cards and to a marked heartbeat class reads, says and taps the card's 4-beat rhythm

Writing – 'Here sits a fat cat', phrase 1 only:

- You tap, class repeats and says rhythm names [see above]
- Each child draws stick notation and one child on a board

Assessing Activity

Spot the composer!

- Child speaks and taps a 4-beat rhythm phrase
- This is written on a board and signed
- Two more are written under the first
- You [later, a child] tap one of the phrases and class identifies the composer

LEARNING OUTCOMES

Children have started:

- using spoken rhythm names
- reading and writing musical notation with simple time symbols

WHAT NEXT?

- Revisit Unit 19 as prep for Unit 28
- Move to Unit 28

Unit 27

HERE SITS A FAT CAT — TRACK 25

soh

Here sits a fat cat, Wait-ing for a fat rat.
No - one came to feed her, poor hun-gry fat cat.

ON A LOG — TRACK 43

soh

On a log, Mis-ter Frog, sang his song the
whole day long: "Croak, croak, croak, croak!"

RAIN, RAIN, GO AWAY — TRACK 49

soh

Rain, rain, go a-way, Come a-gain a-no-ther day.

Unit 28

Three weeks

SKILL AND CONCEPT SEQUENCE

- Performing: improvising
- Concept: pitch

TEACHING OBJECTIVES

- To add a third singing-name, *lah*, to **soh** and **me**
- To work aurally with l-s-m
- To improvise pitch to given rhythm notation

WHAT IS GOING TO HAPPEN?

- Song phrases are sung to singing-names
- The *lah* handsign is introduced
- Melodic phrases are sung to singing-names

KEY SONGS

Key Songs are known <u>before</u> using Teaching Ideas
Italics = first time appearance

- *Bounce high, bounce low*
- Here is the beehive
- Snail, snail
- *Starlight, star bright*
- Tick, tock, see our clock

HOT SONG

- How many miles to Babylon?

TOP TIPS

- In this Unit, pitch will move by 'step' only, ie s – l – s / s – m – s, NOT m – l
- Handsigns and singing-names link the physical and aural memories: they need each other!
- When a child improvises with **incorrect singing-names**, class hums the child's sounds and the child is helped to make the correction(s)
- Use Key Songs to 'tune up', sometimes retuning higher or lower to 'freshen up'

TEACHING IDEAS

Set One

'Tick, tock, see our clock'

Class sings phrase 1 and gestures pitch-changes thus:

'Tick tock tick tock see our clock'
shoulder knee shoulder knee shoulder HEAD shoulder

'Starlight, star bright'

Class sings phrase 1 and gestures pitch-changes thus:
'Star ----------light,   star   bright'
shoulder   HEAD   shoulder   knee

'Here is the beehive'

- Class sings phrase 1, using both hands to show pitch-changes, starting with the shoulders
- Using Thinking Voice only, class performs phrase 1 with hands to show the pitch-changes

Set Two

'Bounce high, bounce low'

- Class sings phrase 1 and gestures pitch-changes:
  'Bounce   high   bounce   low'
  shoulder   HEAD   shoulder   knee
- Class repeats phrase 1 and gestures but HUMS
- Class repeats but signs and sings to singing-names:
  soh   lah   soh   me

[mouth level] [eye level]   [chest-top level]

'Tick, tock, see our clock'

- Class sings then hums phrase 1
- Class sings to singing-names and signs:
  soh   me   soh   me   soh   lah   soh

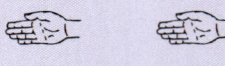

Unit 28

Set Three

Singing-Name Phrases

You sing and sign the examples for class to repeat:

s m s l   s l s m s   s l s l s   s s l l s

The Human Keyboard

Three groups, each assigned a different singing-name in this order:

me   soh   lah

- Class sings with singing-names a phrase from *Set Two* songs to 'tune up'
- You sign same phrase for the groups to sing their assigned singing-name
- An opportunity for individuals to sign

Melodic Phrases

- You say rhythm names for a 4-beat phrase [eg **ta ta ta ta**]; class copies
- You sing and sign:

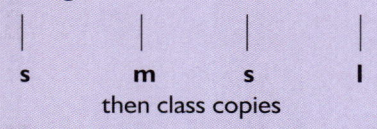

  s   m   s   l

  then class copies

- Use these examples, BUT for the ? s you select a singing-name [improvise]; class copies each example

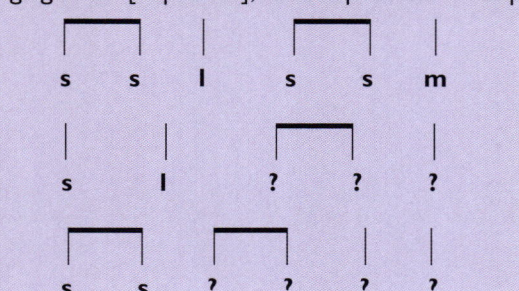

  s s l s s m

  s l ? ? ?

  s s ? ? ? ?

Assessing Activity

'Snail, snail'

- Class sings the song to establish the pitch for **l-s-m**
- Class sings phrases 1 & 2 to singing-names with handsigns [**s-m-s-m**]
- Class sings phrase 3 likewise [**s-s-l-l-s-s-m**]
- Singing-name phrases from *Set Three* are **shown**; class and individuals are invited to sing and sign them

Improvising

- A rhythmic phrase from previous examples is **shown** to class who reads and taps
- Starting on **soh**, a child improvises with **l-s-m** [supported by handsigns] to create a melodic phrase

LEARNING OUTCOMES

- Children have added a crucial link in the singing-names chain
- Children have furthered their skills and understanding of pitch in melody

WHAT NEXT?

- Revisit Unit 27 as prep for Unit 29
- Move to Unit 29

Unit 28

BOUNCE HIGH, BOUNCE LOW — TRACK 2

Bounce high, bounce low, Roll the ball to one you know. (Da - vid) Roll Catch

HERE IS THE BEEHIVE — TRACK 24

Here is the bee-hive, Where are the bees? Hid-den a-way where no-bo-dy sees;
Soon they come creep-ing out of the hive, One, two, three, four, five.

SNAIL, SNAIL — TRACK 52

Snail, Snail, Snail, Snail, Goes a-round and round and round.

STARLIGHT, STAR BRIGHT — TRACK 54

Star - light, star bright, first star I've seen to - night.
Wish I may, wish I might have the wish I wish to - night.

TICK, TOCK, SEE OUR CLOCK — TRACK 58

Tick, tock, tick, tock, see our clock.
Tick, tock, tick, tock, twelve o' clock.

Published by The Voices Foundation and Alfred Publishing Co
© The Voices Foundation 2014

Unit 29

Three/four weeks

SKILL AND CONCEPT SEQUENCE
- Concept: rhythm

TEACHING OBJECTIVES
- To add the **ta rest** [silence] to simple time rhythm

WHAT IS GOING TO HAPPEN?
- The **rest** is found in song phrases
- The **rest** symbol is shown
- Rhythm phrases are read and written

KEY SONGS
Key Songs are known <u>before</u> using Teaching Ideas
Italics = first time appearance
- Bow, wow, wow
- Jelly on a plate
- Mice, mice
- Miss, miss
- Rain is falling down

Key Listening
- The Typewriter

HOT SONG
- Here we go Looby Loo

TOP TIPS
- First impressions need to be the right ones! Plan well, give daily practice, take things gently and ensure success for all – WOW!
- Don't forget, if in doubt, go back to the songs – they've **always** got the answers!

TEACHING IDEAS

Set One
'Bow, wow, wow'
- Class sings song and marks the pulse with tapped heartbeat
- Where there is a 'gap' in the melody, class inserts short single 'woof!'
  "How many 'woofs'?" [3]

'Mice, mice'
- Class says the rhyme and marks the pulse
- Where there is a rhythmic 'gap', the class inserts a short, quiet 'squeak'
  "How many 'squeaks'?" [4]

Set Two
'Rain is falling down'
- Class sings and taps the rhythm
- Where there is a rhythmic 'gap' children insert a 'plop' of rain
- Class repeats twice, but final time the rain has stopped – at each 'gap' class pulls down 'silent' umbrellas

'Miss, miss'
- Class sings and taps the rhythm
- Where there is a silence, each child touches both shoulders
- Repeat, but 'singing' with Thinking Voice

Listening 'The Typewriter'
- In this piece of fast music there are silences [rests] to be found
- The class also listens out for the bell-sound and for when the typewriter carriage is moved across

Unit 29

Set Three

'Jelly on a plate'

- Class chants, taps the rhythm and marks the silences on shoulders

- Class speaks phrases 1 & 2 with rhythm names, taps and marks the silences with fingers on 'sealed lips'

- Phrase 1 is 'written' with Rhythm People thus:

Phrase 2 has same rhythm

teh - teh   **teh - teh**   **ta**   **[silence]**

'Bow, wow, wow'

- Using the same process as 'Jelly on a plate', phrases 1 & 2 only, and finish with class reading:

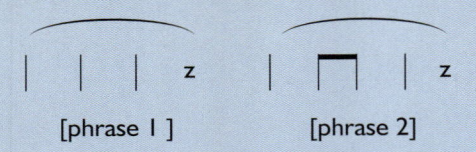

| | | z | ⊓ | z

[phrase 1]   [phrase 2]

Rhythm Cards [On CD]

- You show a card, say *"Off you go!"*; class reads and speaks with rhythm names

- Later class only taps BUT thinks [Thinking Voice] rhythm names

- You show a selection and tap one; class copies and identifies the card; here is an opportunity for individuals to lead

Set Four

'Can you *tap* this rhythm?'

- You sing phrase 1 <u>only</u> and then **tap** a 4-beat phrase [one card-length] of your choice; class **taps** the phrase

'Can you *speak* this rhythm?'

- You sing phrase 1 only and then **tap** a 4-beat [one card-length] phrase of your choice; class performs the phrase using **rhythm names**

'Can you *write* this rhythm?'

- You sing phrase 1 only and then **tap** a 4-beat phrase of your choice

- Class **taps** the phrase

- Class repeats, using **rhythm names**

- **Rhythm People** form the 'stick note' shapes

- Each child **writes** the phrase using stick notation

Assessing Activity

- All three *Set Four* Teaching Ideas are an opportunity for individuals to lead

LEARNING OUTCOMES

- Children are able to tap 4-beat rhythm phrases that include the *rest* [Z], to use the appropriate rhythm names, to read and to write stick-notation

WHAT NEXT?

- Move to Unit 30

BOW, WOW, WOW   TRACK 3

Bow, wow, wow! Whose dog art thou?
Lit - tle Char - lie Chap - lin's dog. Bow, wow, wow!

Unit 29

JELLY ON A PLATE — TRACK 36

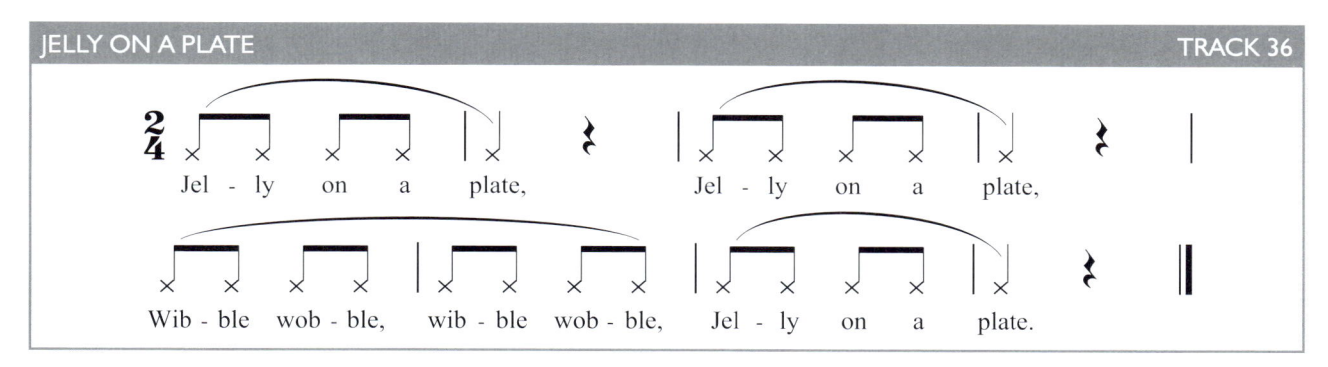

Jel-ly on a plate, Jel-ly on a plate,
Wib-ble wob-ble, wib-ble wob-ble, Jel-ly on a plate.

MICE, MICE — TRACK 41

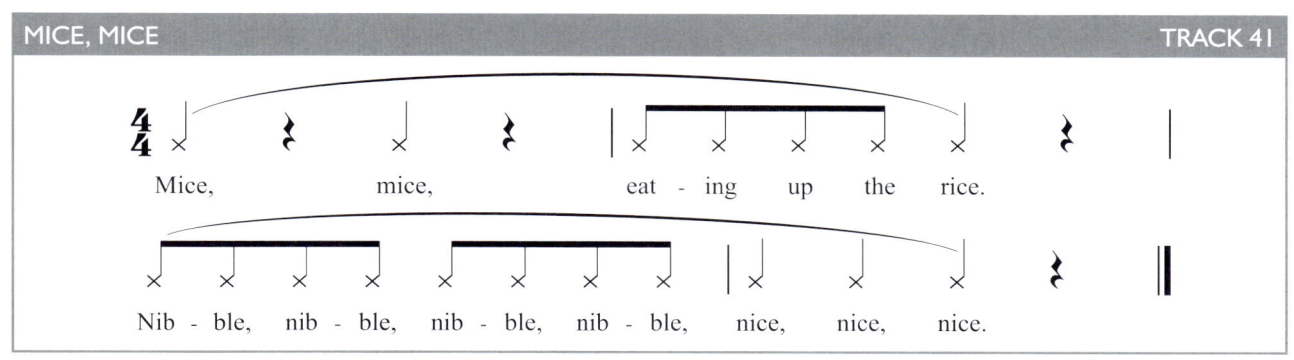

Mice, mice, eat-ing up the rice.
Nib-ble, nib-ble, nib-ble, nib-ble, nice, nice, nice.

MISS, MISS — TRACK 42

soh
Miss, miss, lit-tle miss, miss,
When she miss-es she miss-es like this!

RAIN IS FALLING DOWN — TRACK 47

me
Rain is fal-ling down. Rain is fal-ling down.
Pit-ter, pat-ter, pit-ter, pat-ter, rain is fal-ling down.

Unit 30

Three/four weeks

SKILL AND CONCEPT SEQUENCE
- Performing: singing, playing, improvising
- Concepts: dynamics, phrase, pitch, pulse, rhythm, tempo, timbre
- Listening and thinking

TEACHING OBJECTIVES
- To reinforce performing and listening skills, concepts, games and songs encountered during *First Steps into Music*

WHAT IS GOING TO HAPPEN?
- To employ skills gained and knowledge acquired in songs and activities

KEY SONGS
Key Songs are known *before* using Teaching Ideas
Italics = first time appearance

- *Glowing candlelight*
- Here I come
- Hey, hey, look at me
- I, I, me oh my
- Jelly on a plate
- *Little Johnny dances [Jean Petit il danse]*
- Spinning top
- Starlight, star bright
- Tick, tock, see our clock

Key Listening
- O Polichinelo [Punch]
- A Pobrezinha [Rag Doll]

HOT SONG
- Sing a range of the children's Hot Songs

TOP TIPS
- Pitch: for now, improvised phrases should always start on **soh**

TEACHING IDEAS

Set One: Performing

'Starlight, star bright'
- With 'best singing posture and voices' the class performs consecutively: words – humming – words
- After *"Off you go!"* [starting-pitch and tempo] a large-ish ball is passed round circle in time to the pulse; the class 'sings' phrase 1 with Thinking Voices; the child holding the ball at end of phrase 1 sings phrase 2; the sequence is repeated

'Here I come'
The game is played, but each new leader has to change one or more element – starting pitch, tempo, dynamics

'Jelly on a plate'
Class performs the following sequence:
- Chants and marks the heartbeat [tapped chest]
- Taps on the palm of hand the rhythm sounds, touching shoulders for the silent *rests* [Thinking Voice is used]
- Chants but 'filling' the *rests* with hand-cup 'plops'
- Three groups perform all three body sounds simultaneously [no chant]
- Repeat, minus *rest* sounds
- Repeat, minus *rests* and pulse sounds

Use the above as a basis for an arrangement for percussion

Unit 30

Set Two: Concepts

'I, I, me oh my'

- Class sings the song while marking the heartbeat and with word change:
  '… *how I like my pulse pie*'
- Class sings the song while tapping the rhythm and with word change:
  '… *how I like my rhythm pie*'
- Individuals select pulse or rhythm, then perform and sing the words accordingly
  "*Did the action match the words?*"
  Class repeats or corrects
- Individuals sing '… *how I like my 4-beat pie*' and at the end improvise a 4-beat rhythm phrase, made up from known elements, eg like the rhythm cards

'Spinning top'

- With two rhythm cards selected, two groups each practise one and tap repetitively four times; class now sings the song and at the end, the groups simultaneously perform the rhythms to the song's tempo
- As above but two children each with a different instrument perform

'Tick, tock, see our clock'

- Class sings with the word-change '… *hear our clock, plays this tune at 10 o'clock*'; then the class reads, sings and signs a phrase such as **s-s-m-m** or **s-l-s-m**
- As above but with other 'hours' and other singing-name phrases
- Individuals sing with word-change '… *hear my clock, plays this tune at …*'; then child sings and signs an improvised singing-name phrase

'Hey, hey, look at me'

- Individuals sing with word-change '… *I am* **signing** *can you see?*'; then child starting on **soh** signs a short singing-name phrase for class to sing to

Set Three: Listening and thinking

Listening 'O Polichinelo' [Punch]

- Punch is up to wild mischief! But what?
- Is the class familiar with 'Punch & Judy'?

Listening 'A Pobrezinha' [Rag Doll]

- What does the music tell us about Rag Doll?

'Little Johnny dances' ['Jean Petit il danse']

- NEW song! Teach this French song about the dancing puppet; when class seems secure, together make decisions about the most suitable tempo, dynamics and singing style
- It would be fun to sing it in French!

'Glowing candlelight'

- NEW song! Activity as for previous song

LEARNING OUTCOMES

- Along with the children, you'll realise how much has been achieved by using *First Steps: Age 5-7* over the last two years

WHAT NEXT?

- Have a great summer holiday!

Unit 30

GLOWING CANDLELIGHT
TRACK 17

Glow-ing can-dle-light, Warm and cheer-ful sight.
See the can-dle burn-ing bright-ly, Shin-ing in the night.

HERE I COME
TRACK 23

Here I come! Where from? Bris-tol. What's your trade?
Le-mo-nade. Give us some, don't be a-fraid.

HEY, HEY, LOOK AT ME
TRACK 27

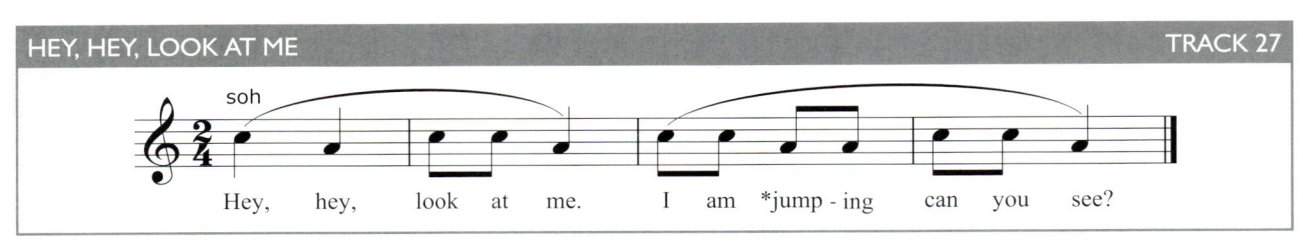

Hey, hey, look at me. I am *jump-ing can you see?

I, I, ME OH MY
TRACK 32

I, I, me oh my, how I like my ap-ple pie.

JELLY ON A PLATE
TRACK 36

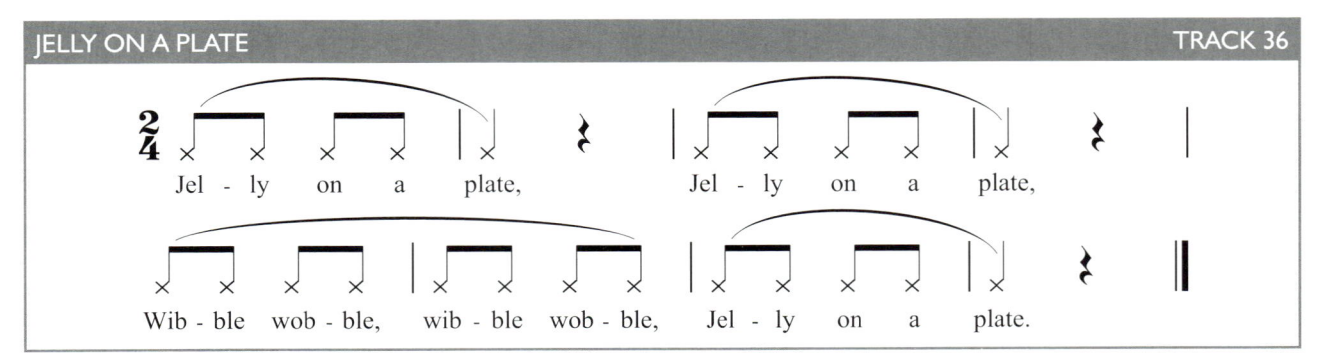

Jel-ly on a plate, Jel-ly on a plate,
Wib-ble wob-ble, wib-ble wob-ble, Jel-ly on a plate.

Unit 30

LITTLE JOHNNY DANCES [JEAN PETIT IL DANSE] — TRACK 38

lah

Lit - tle John - ny dan - ces, on my thumb he dan - ces. Lit - tle John - ny dan - ces, on my thumb he dan - ces. On my thumb, thumb, thumb, Lit - tle John - ny dan - ces.

Jean Pe - tit il dan - se, sur mon pouce il dan - se. Jean Pe - tit il dan - se, sur mon pouce il dan - se. Sur mon pouce, pouce, pouce, Jean Pe - tit il dan - se.

SPINNING TOP — TRACK 53

doh

Spin - ning top goes round and round, Lis - ten to its hum - ming sound.
O - range, yel - low pink and green, Pret - tiest co - lours I have seen.

STARLIGHT, STAR BRIGHT — TRACK 54

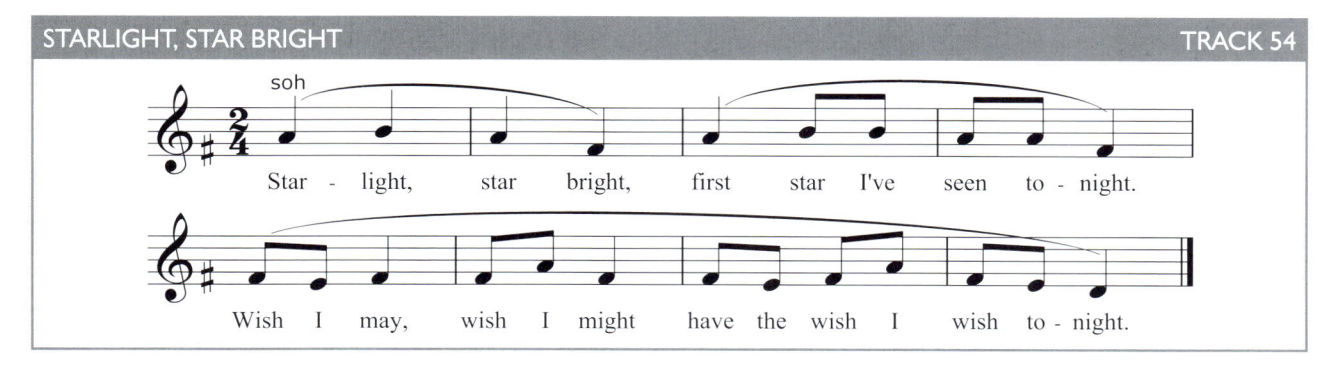

soh

Star - light, star bright, first star I've seen to - night.
Wish I may, wish I might have the wish I wish to - night.

Unit 30

TICK, TOCK, SEE OUR CLOCK
TRACK 58

Tick, tock, tick, tock, see our clock.

Tick, tock, tick, tock, twelve o' clock.

The Songs

Song Index

TITLE	PAGE
A sailor went to sea, sea, sea	117
Bounce high, bounce low	118
Bow, wow, wow	118
Button you must wander	119
Can you tap this rhythm?	120
Can you tap your shoulders?	121
Charlie over the ocean	122
Chest, chest, knee, toe	122
Copy me	123
Doggie, doggie	123
Down came Andrew	124
Down the road	124
Early in the morning	125
Engine, engine	126
Five little monkeys	126
Follow my leader	127
Glowing candlelight	128
Going on a picnic	129
Have you brought?	129
Hello, how are you?	130
Here comes a bluebird	130
Here comes Mrs Macaroni	131
Here I come	131
Here is the beehive	132
Here sits a fat cat	132
Here we go Looby Loo	133
Hey, hey, look at me	133
Hickety tickety	134
How many miles to Babylon?	135
I have a dog	136
I have lost the cupboard key	136
I, I, me oh my	137
I see you	138
Ickle, ockle	139
Jack in the box	139
Jelly on a plate	140
Listen, listen, here I come	140
Little Johnny dances	141
Little Sally Saucer	142
Lots of rosy apples	143
Mice, mice	143
Miss, miss	144
On a log	144
Once a man fell in a well	145
Peter taps with one hammer	145
Pitter, patter	146
Rain is falling down	147
Rain on the green grass	147
Rain, rain, go away	148
Round and round the village	148
Sally go round the sun	149
Snail, snail	149
Spinning top	150
Starlight, star bright	150
Suo gân	151
There was a man	152
Three little birds	152
Tick, tock, see our clock	153
Touch your shoulders	153
Who has the penny?	154
Willum he had seven sons	154

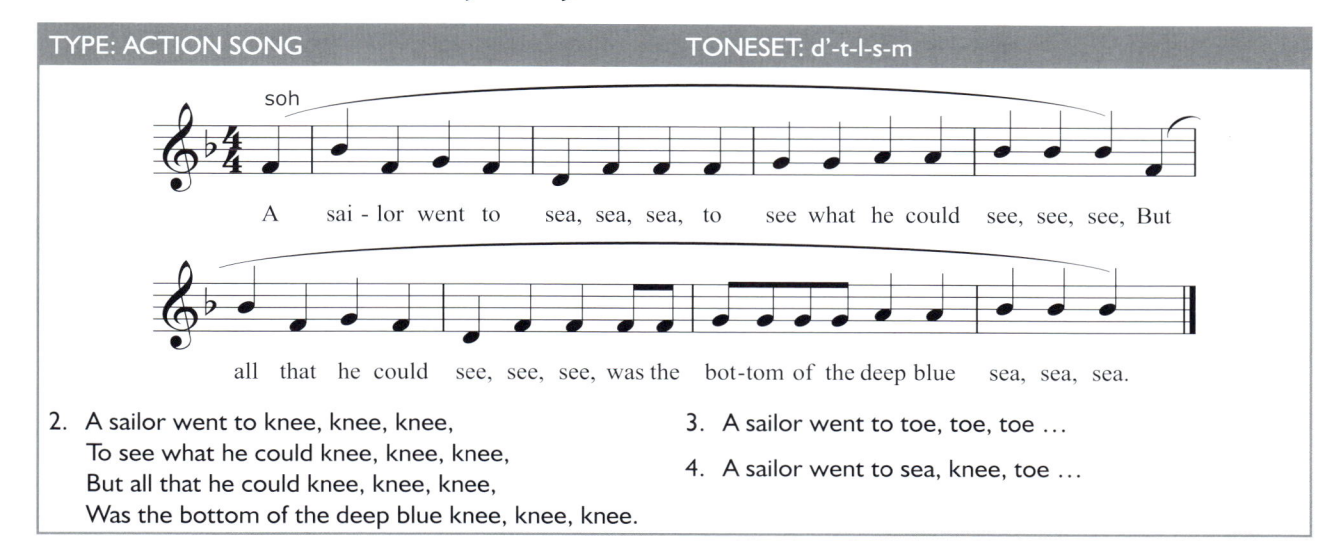

The Songs

A sailor went to sea, sea, sea

TYPE: ACTION SONG **TONESET:** d'-t-l-s-m

[Musical notation: 4/4 time, key of F, beginning on "soh"]

A sai-lor went to sea, sea, sea, to see what he could see, see, see, But all that he could see, see, see, was the bot-tom of the deep blue sea, sea, sea.

2. A sailor went to knee, knee, knee,
   To see what he could knee, knee, knee,
   But all that he could knee, knee, knee,
   Was the bottom of the deep blue knee, knee, knee.

3. A sailor went to toe, toe, toe …

4. A sailor went to sea, knee, toe …

DESCRIPTION OF GAME, ACTION OR ACTIVITY

Each child faces a partner and performs the actions to the pulse:

'(A)	sai -	lor	went	to	sea	sea	sea
	xx	xR	xx	xL	T	T	T
(To)	see	what	he	could	see	see	see
	xx	xR	xx	xL	T	T	T
(But)	all	that	he	could	see	see	see
	xx	xR	xx	xL	T	T	T
(Was the)	bottom	of the	deep	blue	sea	sea	sea'
	xx	xR	xx	xL	T	T	T

Key: xx = clap own hands   xR = right hands slap   xL = left hands slap   T = tap own forehead

For other verses, actions as before BUT for the T:-
- Verse 2: pat knees three times
- Verse 3: touch toes three times
- Verse 4: tap, pat, touch [once each]

Three different instruments:
- Verse 1: for each 'sea' and 'see', instrument A plays
- Verse 2: for each 'knee', instrument B plays
- Verse 3: for each 'toe', instrument C plays
- Verse 4: for each 'sea, knee, toe', instruments A B C [once each]

The class uses the Thinking Voice when the instruments play.

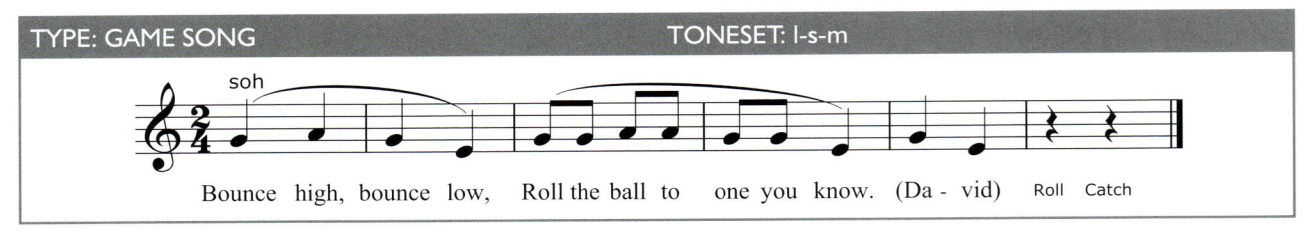

Bounce high, bounce low

TYPE: GAME SONG	TONESET: l-s-m

Bounce high, bounce low, Roll the ball to one you know. (Da-vid) Roll Catch

DESCRIPTION OF GAME, ACTION OR ACTIVITY

The class forms a circle, with one child in the centre holding a medium-size ball. This person bounces the ball each time the word 'bounce' is sung. Child 1 selects the next child by singing his or her name at the end. The ball is immediately rolled to the new person who goes with the ball to the centre and the game is repeated.

Singing Development: The solo singer is required to pitch-match the rest of the class.

Bow, wow, wow

TYPE: GAME SONG	TONESET: l-s-m-r-d

Bow, wow, wow! Whose dog art thou? Lit-tle Char-lie Chap-lin's dog. Bow, wow, wow!

DESCRIPTION OF GAME, ACTION OR ACTIVITY

Standing in a circle, each child faces a partner and performs actions as follows:

Bow, wow, wow	With both hands held at about shoulder height and palms facing forward, the partners slap each other's hands three times to the pulse ('high five' style).
Whose dog art thou?	Each child points and wags a finger to the pulse.
Little Charlie Chaplin's dog	The partners swing each other with linked arms or hands so as to exchange places.
Bow, wow, wow	The partners slap hands three times in 'high five' style as before and then immediately jump and spin round on the spot. Each child now faces a new partner and the game can begin again.

Singing Challenge: Can the children maintain the singing with as much quality as possible while simultaneously carrying out the actions?

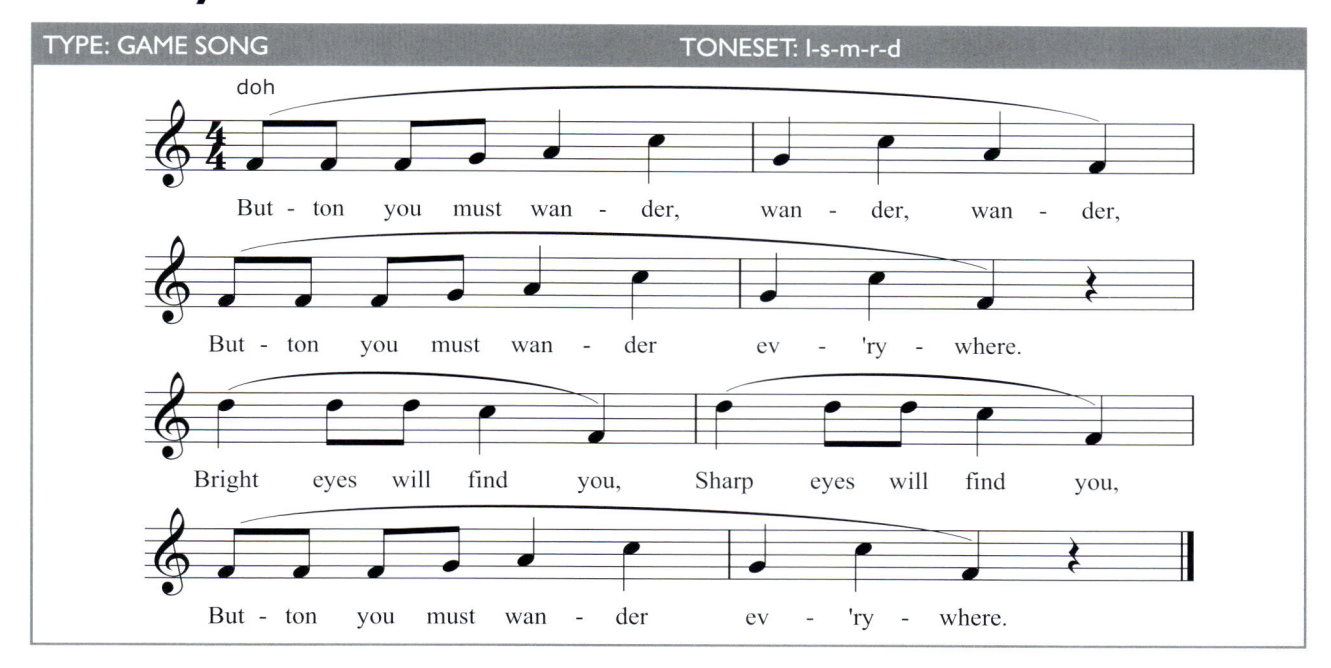

Button you must wander

TYPE: GAME SONG **TONESET: l-s-m-r-d**

Button you must wander, wander, wander,
Button you must wander ev-'ry-where.
Bright eyes will find you, Sharp eyes will find you,
Button you must wander ev-'ry-where.

DESCRIPTION OF GAME, ACTION OR ACTIVITY

The children stand in a circle with both hands outstretched in front, the back of each hand uppermost, holding on to a loop of string which goes round the entire circle. During the singing of the song, a button (or similar) that has been threaded on the string is passed covertly from hand to hand round the circle. A child standing in the centre tries to detect who has the button at the end of the song.

Singing Development: The children need to approach the singing of the third phrase with an awareness of 'high' thinking, a 'tall' posture and lots of tummy support.

Can you tap this rhythm?

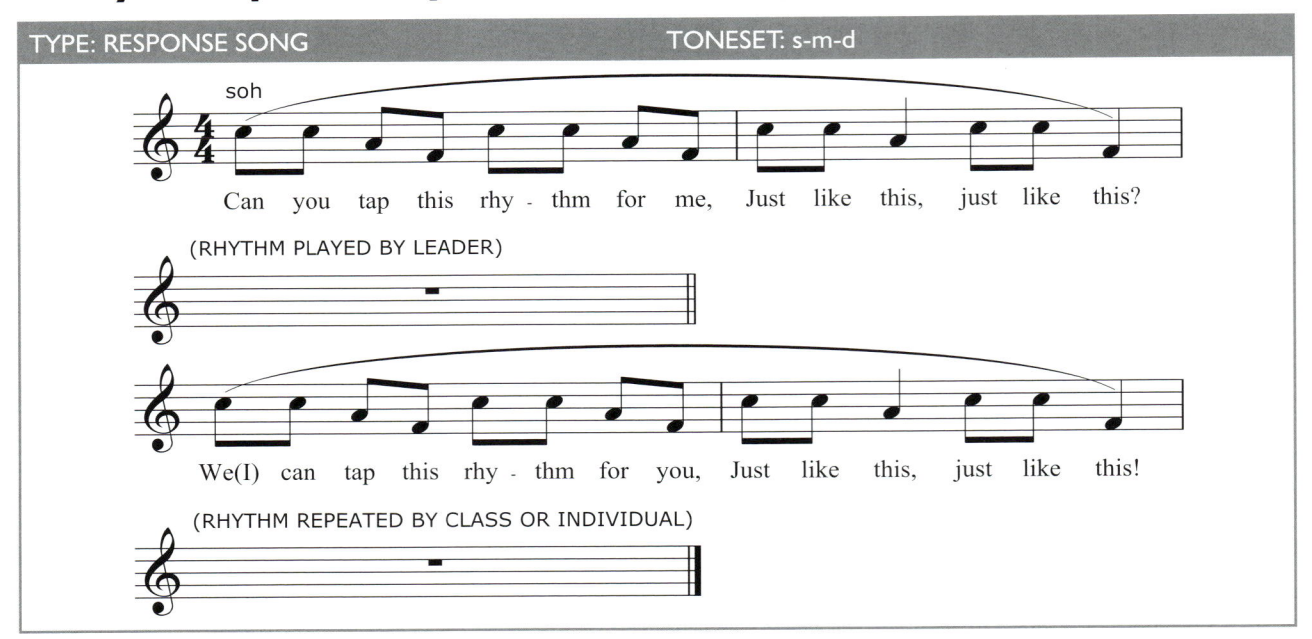

TYPE: RESPONSE SONG **TONESET:** s-m-d

[Musical notation: Phrase 1 with lyrics "Can you tap this rhy-thm for me, Just like this, just like this?" starting on soh, followed by (RHYTHM PLAYED BY LEADER) on empty staff.]

[Musical notation: Phrase 2 with lyrics "We(I) can tap this rhy-thm for you, Just like this, just like this!" followed by (RHYTHM REPEATED BY CLASS OR INDIVIDUAL) on empty staff.]

DESCRIPTION OF GAME, ACTION OR ACTIVITY

The leader of the game sings the question followed by a 4-beat improvised rhythm phrase within the same tempo. The class [or group or individual] either:

immediately responds by copying the given rhythm and then sings phrase 2

or:

sings phrase 2 first and then performs the rhythm phrase – this is much more challenging

Additional listening and thinking skills can be added to the game, for example:

the leader performs the phrase with consciously considered dynamics that the class must replicate; if the leader considers the phrase has not been replicated accurately then, without saying why, he/she immediately performs the same phrase once more for the class to try again.

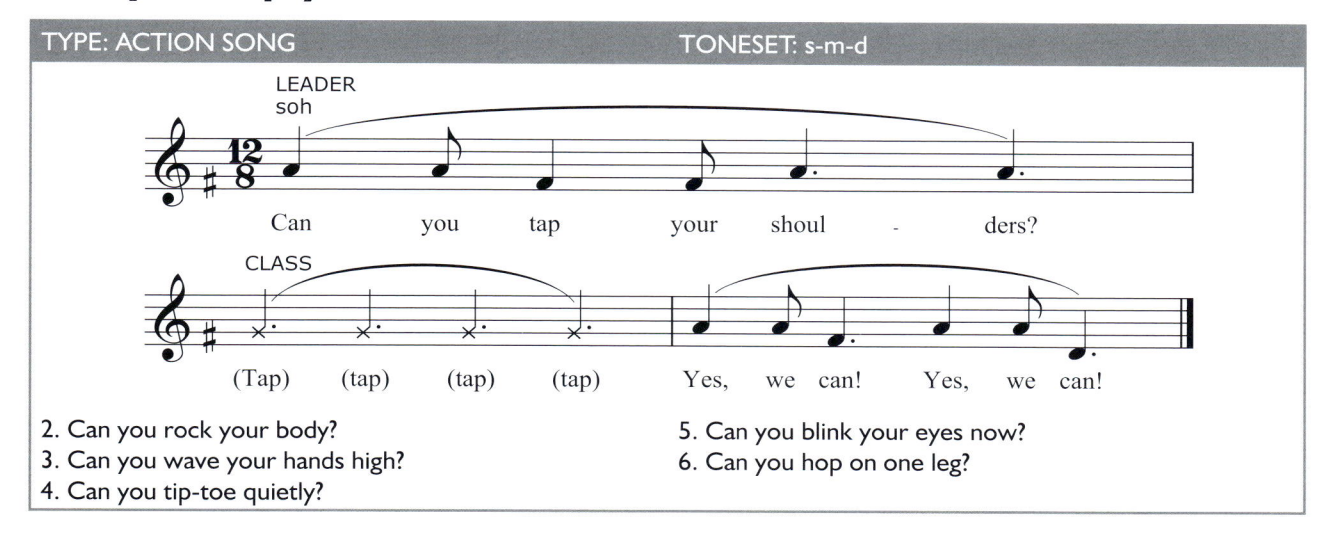

Can you tap your shoulders?

TYPE: ACTION SONG   **TONESET:** s-m-d

LEADER: Can you tap your shoul-ders?
CLASS: (Tap) (tap) (tap) (tap) Yes, we can! Yes, we can!

2. Can you rock your body?
3. Can you wave your hands high?
4. Can you tip-toe quietly?
5. Can you blink your eyes now?
6. Can you hop on one leg?

DESCRIPTION OF GAME, ACTION OR ACTIVITY

A leader chooses an action and sings the opening question of the song. The class performs the action four times (with the pulse) and sings the final response. This song helps the children to recognise that music involves listening, waiting, coming in at the correct time and performing with accuracy.

Singing Development: These activities provide opportunities for the children to gain confidence in individual singing and leadership.

Charlie over the ocean

TYPE: GAME SONG **TONESET: m-r-d-l,-s,**

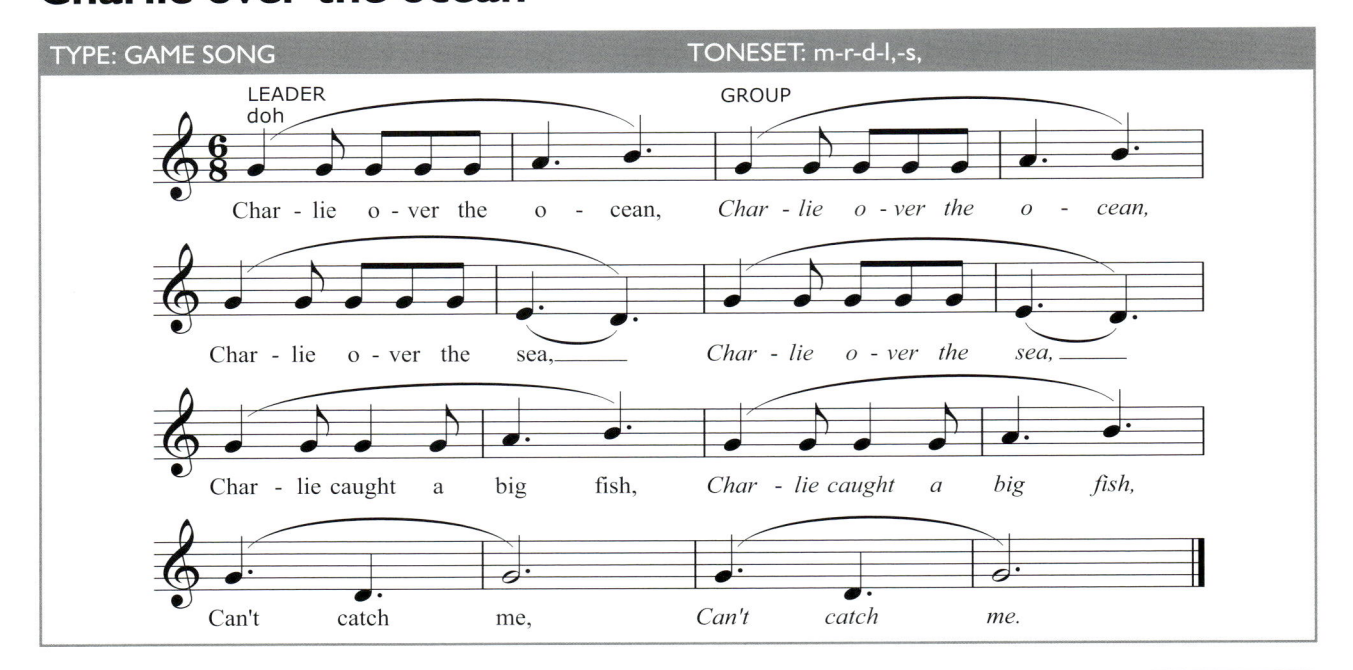

(LEADER) Charlie over the ocean, *(GROUP)* Charlie over the ocean,
Charlie over the sea, Charlie over the sea,
Charlie caught a big fish, Charlie caught a big fish,
Can't catch me, Can't catch me.

DESCRIPTION OF GAME, ACTION OR ACTIVITY

The children form a circle. Carrying a toy fish or a suitable object, the leader walks round the outside of the circle singing the song [Call]. Each phrase is echoed by the group [Response]. The leader drops the fish behind someone and runs round the circle. The chosen person quickly picks up the fish and runs after the leader, trying to catch him before he reaches the vacant space in the circle.

Chest, chest, knee, toe

TYPE: ACTION SONG **TONESET: l-s-m-r-d**

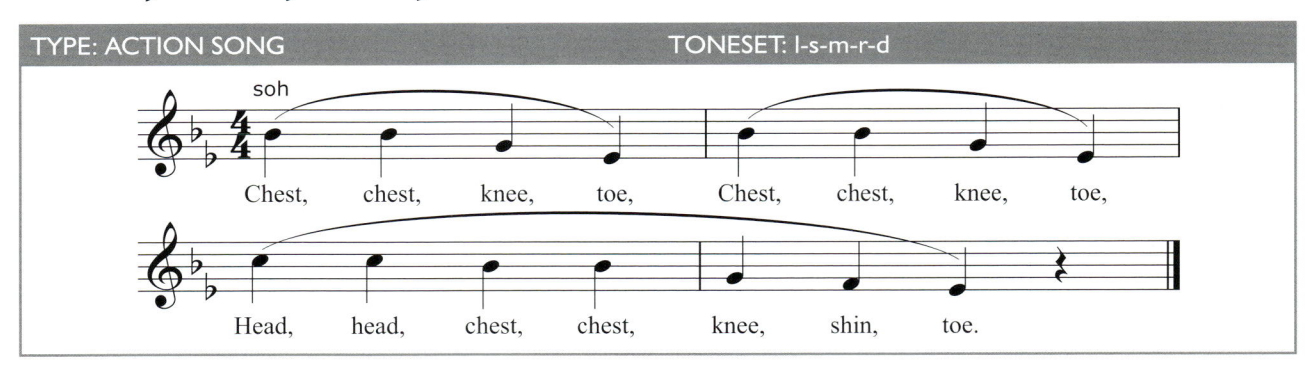

Chest, chest, knee, toe, Chest, chest, knee, toe,
Head, head, chest, chest, knee, shin, toe.

DESCRIPTION OF GAME, ACTION OR ACTIVITY

With both hands, the children touch the part of the body indicated by the words of the song as they sing.

Copy me

TYPE: ACTION SONG **TONESET: l-s-f-m-r-d**

Co-py me, co-py me, You can do it too! Co-py me, co-py me, Then I'll co-py you.

DESCRIPTION OF GAME, ACTION OR ACTIVITY

Everyone sits in a circle. The leader – in the first instance the teacher – sings the song and makes up two different actions, one for each phrase. Choose actions that will move easily with the pulse, eg tapping, waving, rocking. The children join in with the actions.

Now ask a child to choose two different actions and perform them as you sing.

Individuals sing the song and perform their chosen actions. The class repeats the song and the actions.

Doggie, doggie

TYPE: GAME SONG **TONESET: l-s-m**

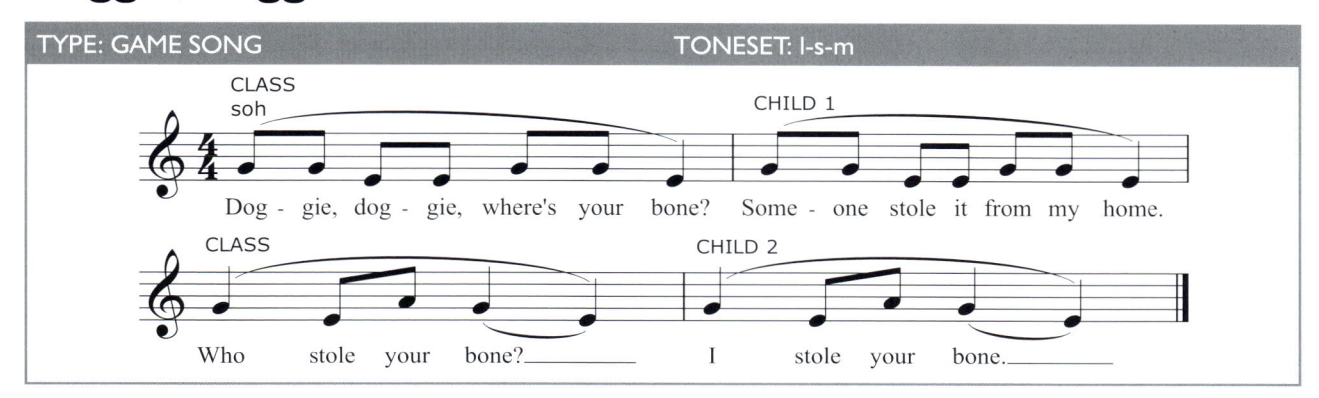

CLASS: *Dog-gie, dog-gie, where's your bone?* CHILD 1: *Some-one stole it from my home.*
CLASS: *Who stole your bone?* CHILD 2: *I stole your bone.*

DESCRIPTION OF GAME, ACTION OR ACTIVITY

The children sit in a circle. A child is invited to be the 'doggie' and sits in the 'kennel' in the centre of the circle – or elsewhere – but unable to see the children in the circle. Another child is quietly chosen to hold the 'bone' and to conceal it.

The class sings the first phrase and the 'doggie' replies. The class sings the third phrase and the child holding the 'bone' responds. By listening carefully to the Singing Voice, the 'doggie' identifies the child who has the bone.

If the children find this activity too easy, the child with the 'bone' might be asked to disguise her Singing Voice. A further challenge for the 'doggie' would be to employ two bones, with the 'bone' children singing their responses simultaneously.

Singing Challenge: The 'doggie' and 'bone' children should be expected to pitch-match the rest of the singing even when trying to disguise their voices.

Down came Andrew

TYPE: GAME SONG **TONESET: s-m-r-d**

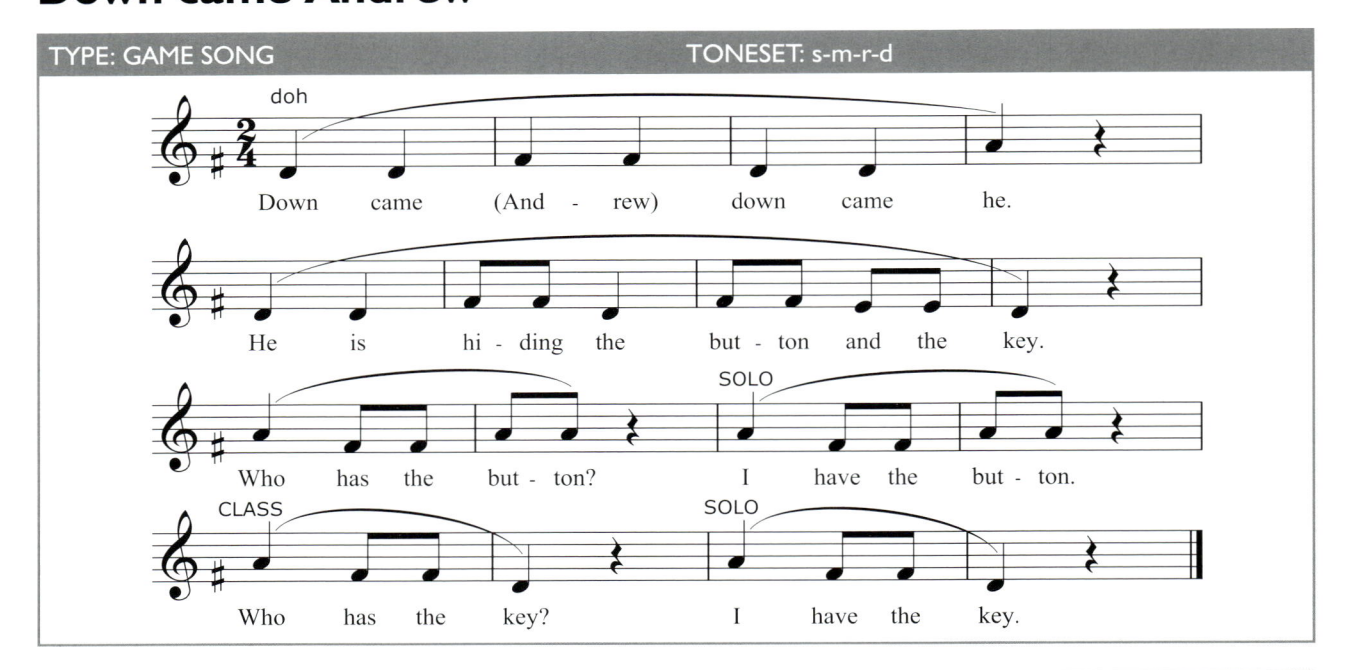

Down came (Andrew) down came he.
He is hiding the button and the key.
Who has the button? (SOLO) I have the button.
(CLASS) Who has the key? (SOLO) I have the key.

DESCRIPTION OF GAME, ACTION OR ACTIVITY

The children stand in a circle with their hands behind their backs. A child is selected to go to the centre and close eyes. During the singing of the first two phrases, another child, whose name is used in the song, goes round the outside of the circle and gives the key to one person and the button to another. Everyone sings, 'Who has the button?' and the relevant child sings back; likewise, the key. The 'hiding' child has to identify from the sounds of the voices who has the button and who has the key.

Singing Challenge: The children with the button and key should pitch-match the pitch of the class singing.

Down the road

TYPE: ACTION SONG **TONESET: m-r-d-l,-s,**

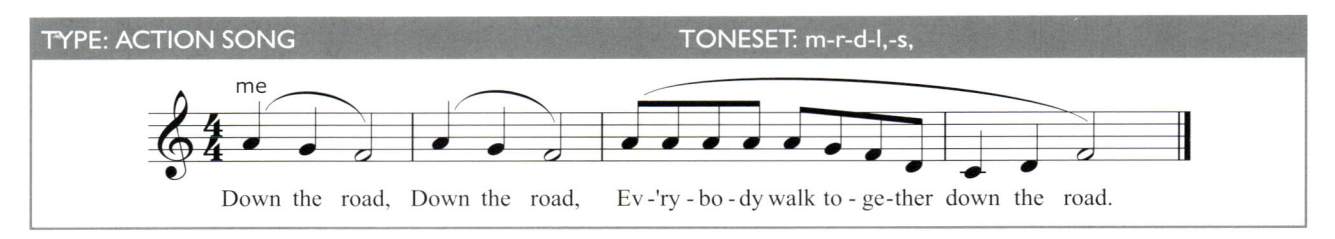

Down the road, Down the road, Ev-'ry-bo-dy walk to-ge-ther down the road.

DESCRIPTION OF GAME, ACTION OR ACTIVITY

This is a song requiring children to work co-operatively, eg walking in a circle or line.

Other actions can be asked for by replacing "walk" with "wave" or "sway". "Walk together" might be replaced by "moving quietly" or "marching loudly".

Other verses might be invented, such as, "Time to work, time to work, Everybody settle down, It's time to work" or "Story time, story time, Everybody come together, Story time".

All actions should be done to the feel of the pulse. The tempo [speed] and dynamics [volume] of the singing should reflect the words.

Early in the morning

TYPE: GAME SONG **TONESET: l-s-f-m-r-d**

soh

Ear - ly in the mor - ning at eight o' - clock,

you can hear the post - man knock.

Up jumps John to o - pen the door.

One let - ter, two let - ters, three let - ters, four.

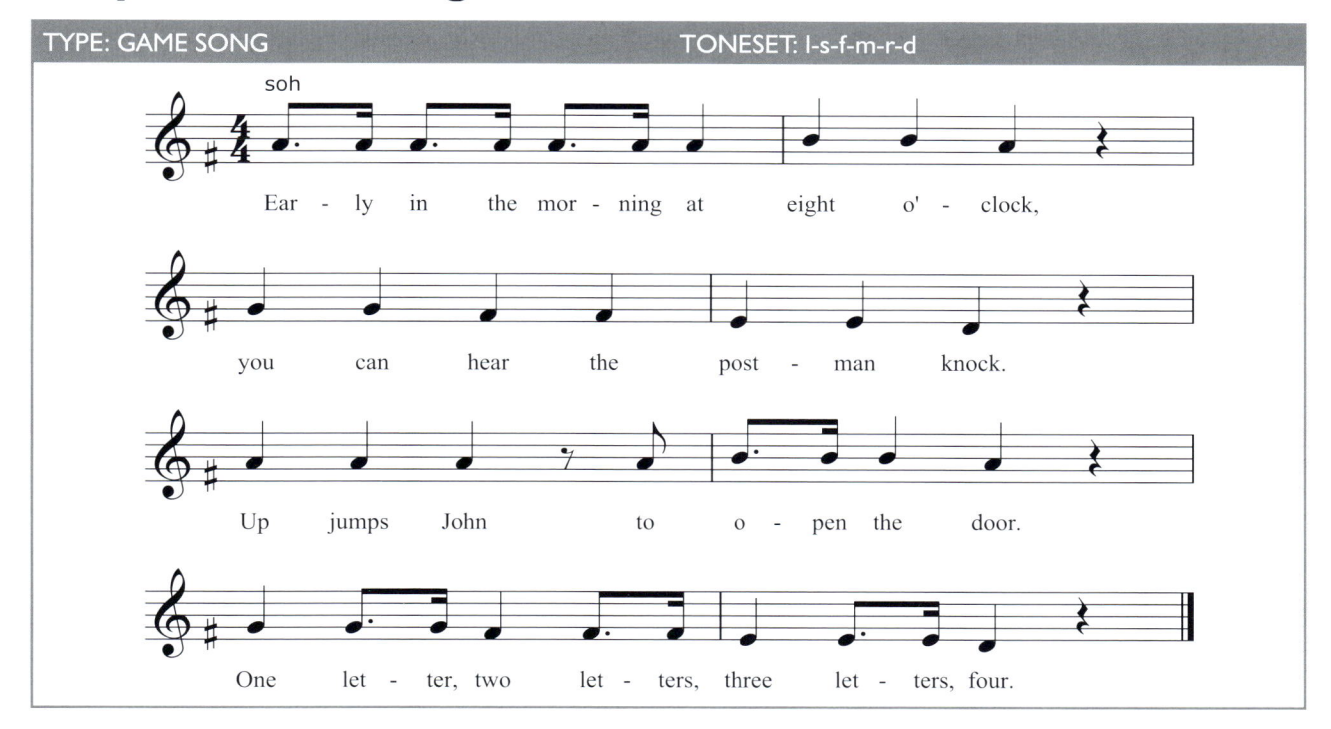

DESCRIPTION OF GAME, ACTION OR ACTIVITY

Sit or stand in a circle. The 'postman' walks around close to the children until "postman knock", when he stops in front of someone and 'knocks on the door'. The chosen child 'opens the door' and the postman delivers four letters as the four numbers are sung.

The tempo of the song could be varied according to how energetic the postman is feeling!

Consider using instruments to play with "postman knock" and at "**one** letter, **two** letters, **three** letters, **four**"

Published by The Voices Foundation and Alfred Publishing Co
© The Voices Foundation 2014

Engine, engine

TYPE: SONG **TONESET: l-s-m-r-d**

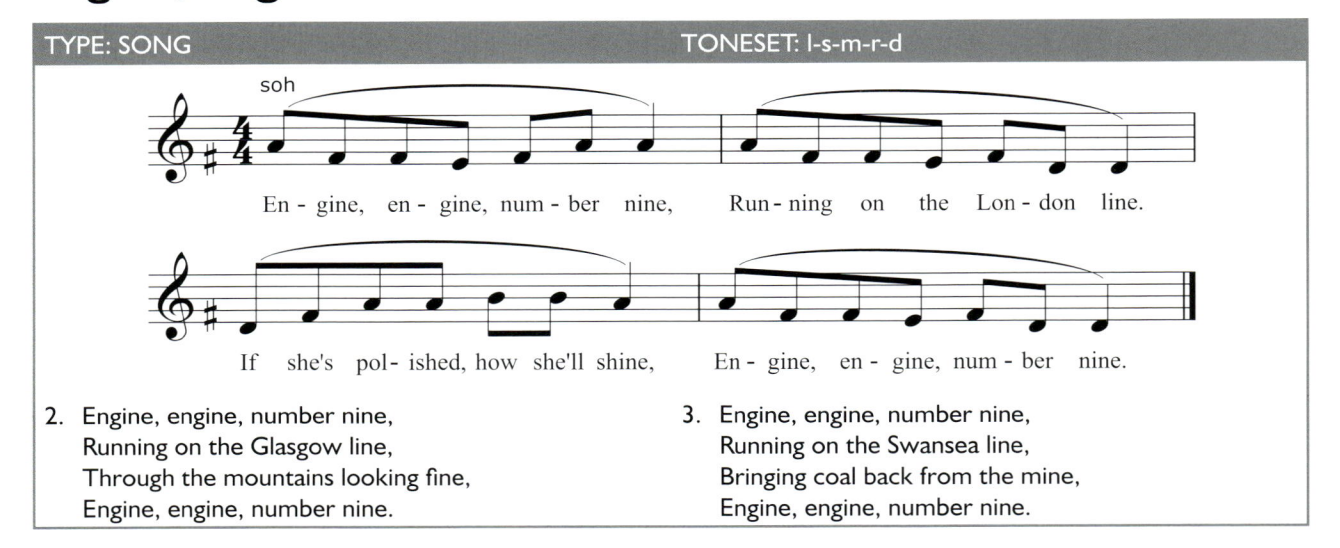

Engine, engine, number nine,
Running on the London line.
If she's polished, how she'll shine,
Engine, engine, number nine.

2. Engine, engine, number nine,
   Running on the Glasgow line,
   Through the mountains looking fine,
   Engine, engine, number nine.

3. Engine, engine, number nine,
   Running on the Swansea line,
   Bringing coal back from the mine,
   Engine, engine, number nine.

DESCRIPTION OF GAME, ACTION OR ACTIVITY

A line of children (the 'train') prepares to sing the song and walk to the pulse while singing. The leader (the 'engine') sings the first phrase to establish the tempo and pitch before the 'train' leaves the station singing the rest of the song. The tempo should be varied for each new performance to suit the new speed of the 'train'.

Show the children that this melody has four equal-length phrases. By agreement in advance, the 'train' sings the song with Singing Voices, except for phrase 2 (Thinking Voices) when the train goes into a tunnel. In this way, other phrases might be used as 'tunnel phrases'. For example, a very long tunnel might need two, or more, phrases.

Singing Development: Make sure the children 'scale the heights' of the rising pitch of phrase 3 by suggesting that they look into the distance to see if the train is coming! In this way the pitch-thinking is better placed and ensures correct tuning.

Five little monkeys

TYPE: ACTION SONG **TONESET: l-s-m**

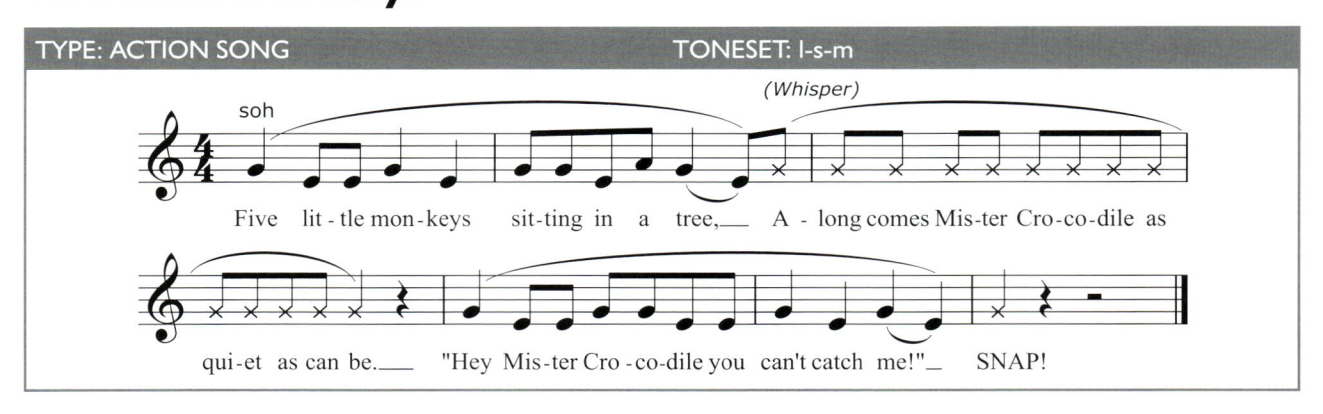

Five little monkeys sitting in a tree,
Along comes Mister Crocodile as (Whisper)
quiet as can be.
"Hey Mister Crocodile you can't catch me!"
SNAP!

DESCRIPTION OF GAME, ACTION OR ACTIVITY

The children show five 'little monkey' fingers on one hand. With the other hand they make the action of a crocodile snapping. During phrase 3 the 'crocodile' hand moves nearer and nearer until "SNAP!" The crocodile eats one of the monkeys, leaving only four in the tree. Repeat until there are no monkeys left.

Follow my leader

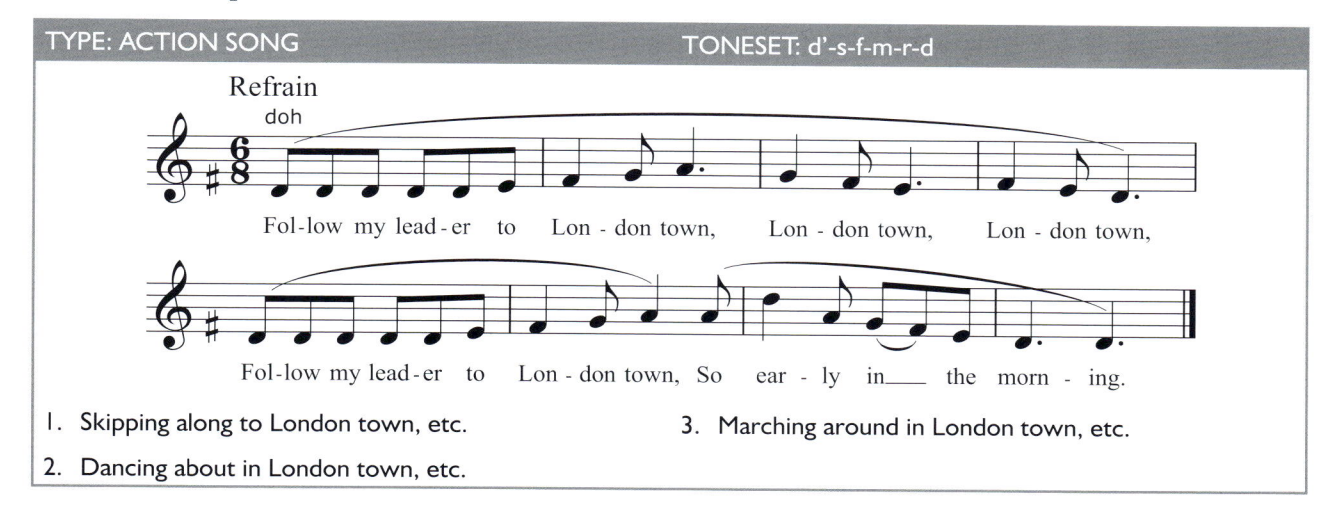

TYPE: ACTION SONG **TONESET: d'-s-f-m-r-d**

Refrain

Fol-low my lead-er to Lon-don town, Lon-don town, Lon-don town,
Fol-low my lead-er to Lon-don town, So ear-ly in the morn-ing.

1. Skipping along to London town, etc.
2. Dancing about in London town, etc.
3. Marching around in London town, etc.

DESCRIPTION OF GAME, ACTION OR ACTIVITY

Children form a line behind the leader. Before moving everyone sings the Refrain. The leader then moves off followed by the others, singing a verse he has selected. Quickly the followers join in with both words and movement. Which movement will the leader select?

Glowing candlelight

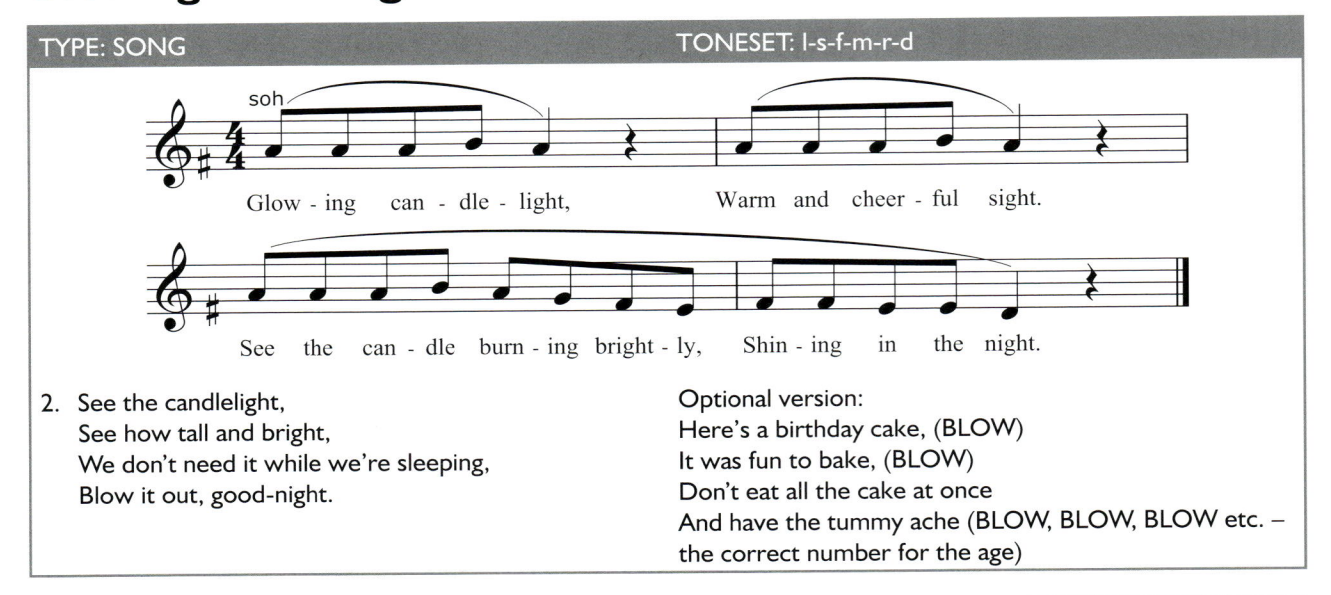

TYPE: SONG **TONESET: l-s-f-m-r-d**

[Musical notation with lyrics:]
Glow-ing can-dle-light, Warm and cheer-ful sight.
See the can-dle burn-ing bright-ly, Shin-ing in the night.

2. See the candlelight,
   See how tall and bright,
   We don't need it while we're sleeping,
   Blow it out, good-night.

Optional version:
Here's a birthday cake, (BLOW)
It was fun to bake, (BLOW)
Don't eat all the cake at once
And have the tummy ache (BLOW, BLOW, BLOW etc. – the correct number for the age)

DESCRIPTION OF GAME, ACTION OR ACTIVITY

Singing Development: The singing should suggest the gentleness and warmth of the candle flame. To do this it is necessary to ask for quieter and *legato (smooth)* style of singing. The sound should not be breathy but requires full-strength support from the diaphragm, and a focus of delivery from the cheek-eye-forehead area of the face.

For the first verse, ask the children to hold up three fingers of one hand to represent candles. As they sing, one candle is 'blown out' at each musical *rest* and one finger is tucked away. In verse 2, four 'finger-candles' are needed. The third 'blow' interrupts the melody before the singing of "good-night" and a final 'blow'.

In the optional version, the number of fingers held up depends on the child's birthday. One 'finger-candle' is blown out at the end of each of the first two phrases, and the remainder with blows for each of the remaining candles at the end of the verse.

As an alternative activity, individual standing children could represent the candles. In the birthday cake verse, the appropriate number of candles could stand in the middle of a circle, with the birthday child blowing out the candles.

Going on a picnic

TYPE: RESPONSE SONG **TONESET: s-m-r-d-s,-l,**

(musical notation)

Go-ing on a pic-nic, leav-ing right a-way. If it does-n't rain we'll stay all day. Have you brought the ap-ple?
SOLO: Yes, I've brought the ap-ple. Go-ing on a pic-nic on a love-ly day.

DESCRIPTION OF GAME, ACTION OR ACTIVITY

Build up the verses by adding other food and drink to the picnic basket. When a list has been built, individuals can be organised to sing the solo phrases.

Individuals can sing phrase 3 selecting randomly from the list with the class singing the answer.

As for the above activity, but the picnic basket list is committed to memory and items randomly selected. Ideally there should be no interruption or hesitation when singing the question and answers.

Have you brought?

TYPE: RESPONSE SONG **TONESET: s-m**

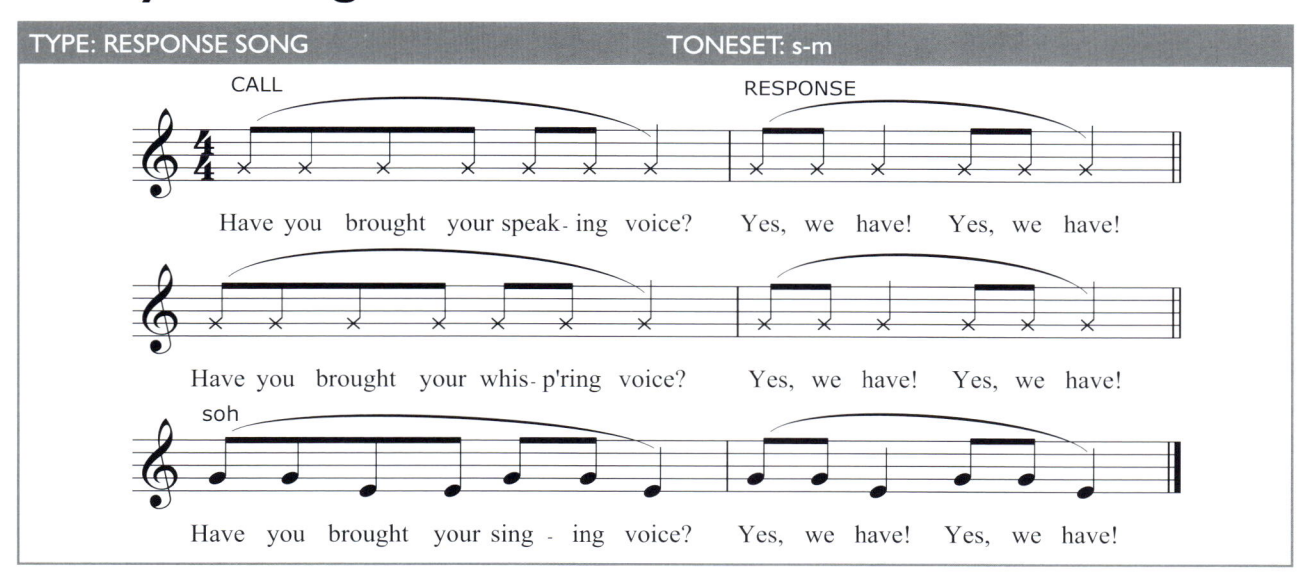

CALL: Have you brought your speak-ing voice? RESPONSE: Yes, we have! Yes, we have!
Have you brought your whis-p'ring voice? Yes, we have! Yes, we have!
Have you brought your sing-ing voice? Yes, we have! Yes, we have!

DESCRIPTION OF GAME, ACTION OR ACTIVITY

This activity is of significant importance, particularly for those children who have not yet found their Singing Voice and do not understand the distinction we all need to make between singing and speaking. Most children find their Singing Voice instinctively but, occasionally, some children try to sing with a speaking voice! So this activity is useful for helping children to distinguish the different capabilities of the voice, and to give practice in finding and using these.

Hello, how are you?

TYPE: RESPONSE SONG	TONESET: s-m

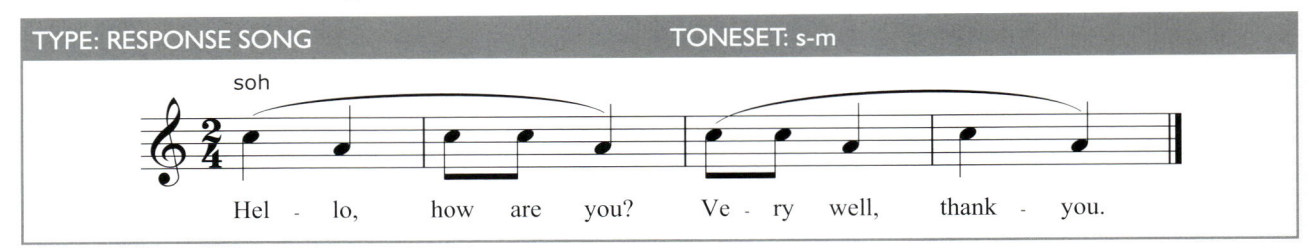

soh
Hel-lo, how are you? Ve-ry well, thank-you.

DESCRIPTION OF GAME, ACTION OR ACTIVITY

This is a simple greeting song between teacher and children, teacher and child, and child and class. It is particularly helpful to use this song as a greeting between two children, because it gives confidence to children in performing on their own in front of others.

The children might be encouraged to devise other sung greetings – and also farewells.

Here comes a bluebird

TYPE: GAME SONG	TONESET: l-s-m-r-d

soh
Here comes a blue-bird through the win-dow, Hey, did-dle dum a day, day, day.
Take a lit-tle part-ner, hop in the gar-den, Hey, did-dle dum a day, day, day.

DESCRIPTION OF GAME, ACTION OR ACTIVITY

A circle is formed with joined hands. One child (the 'bird') walks outside the circle until, on the word "window", he enters the circle by passing through joined hands held high. On "Take a little partner" the 'bird' selects another child from the circle and, with both of their hands joined, they face each other and gallop sideways out and back again through the opening left by the chosen child. The second child now becomes the new 'bird' for repeating the song.

Singing Challenge: Ask the children to maintain the quality of their singing while the game takes place. This should be achieved without teacher support.

Here comes Mrs Macaroni

TYPE: GAME SONG **TONESET:** s-f-m-r-d-t,-s,

doh

Here comes Miss-is Ma-ca-ro-ni, Ri-ding on her milk-white po-ny,

Here she comes with all her mo-ney, Miss-is Ma-ca-ro-ni. Hong- Kong, Hong- Kong,

Su-zy-an-na, Hong- Kong, Hong- Kong, Su-zy-an-na,

Hong- Kong, Hong- Kong, Su-zy-an-na, Miss-is Ma-ca-ro-ni.

DESCRIPTION OF GAME, ACTION OR ACTIVITY

The game is played at a lively pace. A child stands in the centre of a circle of children skipping around and singing. At the end of phrase 2, the child chooses a partner. For phrases 3 and 4, the circle stands still and claps the couple skipping around inside the circle, holding crossed hands.

Here I come

TYPE: GAME SONG **TONESET:** s-m

soh

Here I come! Where from? Bris-tol. What's your trade?

Le-mo-nade. Give us some, don't be a-fraid.

DESCRIPTION OF GAME, ACTION OR ACTIVITY

The leader – the Lemonade Man – sings "Here I come"; the class responds with "Where from?" The song continues in this alternating 'call-and-response' style. At the end of the song, every child holds out a pretend glass and the Lemonade Man pours a drink into the glass of one outstretched hand – this selects the next Lemonade Man and the game continues.

Singing Development: The leader sets the starting pitch, tempo and dynamics for the others to replicate. Encourage the leader to consider these before starting.

Here is the beehive

TYPE: ACTION SONG **TONESET: l-s-m-r-d**

Here is the bee-hive, Where are the bees? Hid-den a-way where no-bo-dy sees;
Soon they come creep-ing out of the hive, One, two, three, four, five.

DESCRIPTION OF GAME, ACTION OR ACTIVITY

One hand is held in the shape of a beehive and the fingers of the other hand are tucked inside during the singing of the first three phrases. As the last phrase is sung, the 'bees' emerge one at a time and, after the song is finished, fly around making a buzzing sound.

A group of, say, twelve children form a standing horseshoe shape with arms raised to make a roof that resembles a beehive. The five 'bees' crouch inside the hive and emerge to fly around with a buzzing sound at the end of the song.

Here sits a fat cat

TYPE: GAME SONG **TONESET: l-s-m**

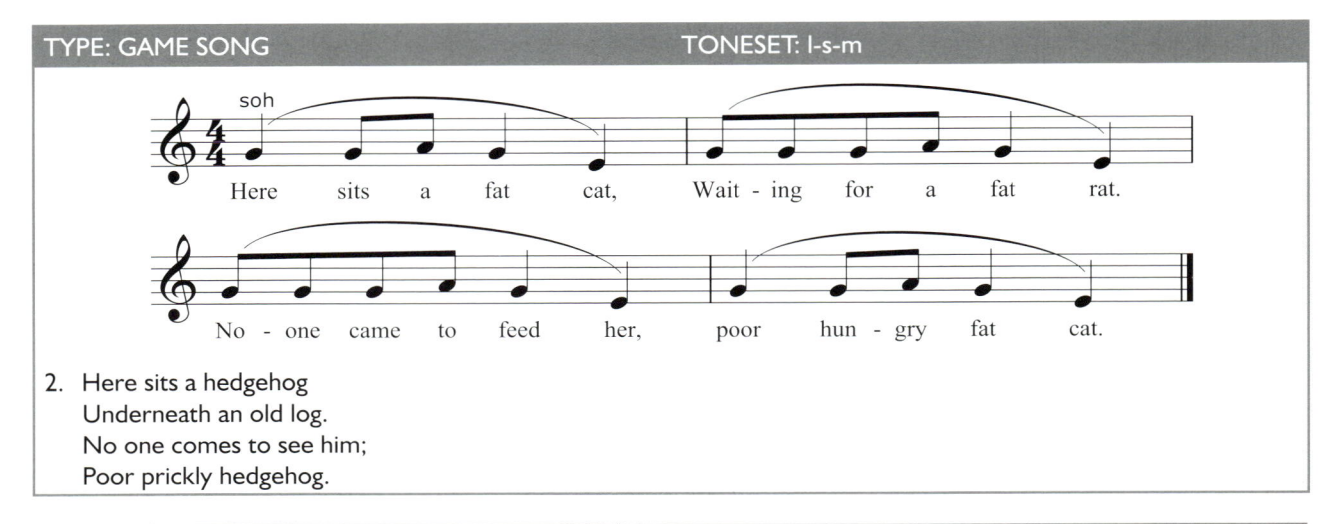

Here sits a fat cat, Wait-ing for a fat rat.
No-one came to feed her, poor hun-gry fat cat.

2. Here sits a hedgehog
   Underneath an old log.
   No one comes to see him;
   Poor prickly hedgehog.

DESCRIPTION OF GAME, ACTION OR ACTIVITY

The children sit as a circle. One child is selected to be the 'fat cat' curled up in the middle of the circle, with closed eyes. A set of small bells, or similar, is placed behind the 'cat'. As the song is sung, a selected child creeps up and quietly takes the bells back to his place, hiding them from sight. At the end of the song the 'cat' has to guess who stole the bells. The second verse can be used in the same way.

Singing Development: The song is sung gently and quietly so as not to disturb the 'fat cat'.

Here we go Looby Loo

TYPE: ACTION SONG **TONESET: l-s-f-m-r-d**

Refrain: Here we go Loo-by Loo, Here we go Loo-by Light, Here we go Loo-by Loo, All on a Sa-tur-day night.

1. You put your right arm in, You put your right arm out, You shake it a lit-tle, a lit-tle, And turn your-self a-bout. [Back to Refrain]

2. You put your *left arm* in, etc.
3. You put your *right leg* in, etc.
4. You put your *left leg* in, etc.
5. You put your *whole self* in, etc.

DESCRIPTION OF GAME, ACTION OR ACTIVITY

During the Refrain, the children skip round in a circle. They stand still for the verses, carrying out the appropriate action as suggested by the words.

Hey, hey, look at me

TYPE: ACTION SONG **TONESET: s-m**

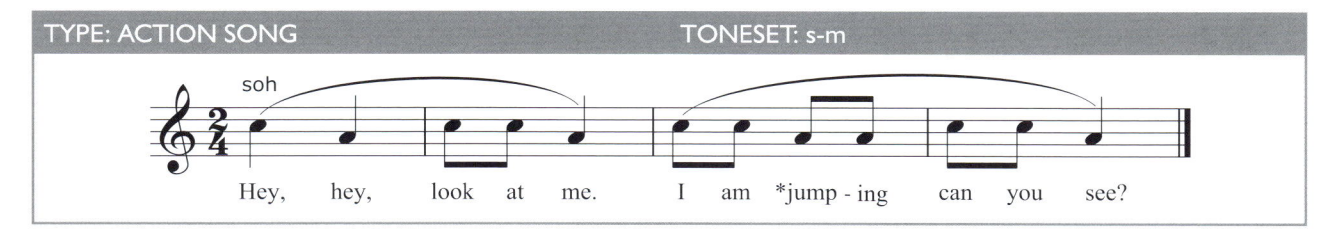

Hey, hey, look at me. I am *jump-ing can you see?

DESCRIPTION OF GAME, ACTION OR ACTIVITY

A child sings and during "I am [eg tapping], can you see?" performs a chosen action in time with the pulse. The class repeats by pitch-matching the leader and replicating the same tempo, dynamic and action. Other possible action words: 'waving', 'hopping', 'patting', 'winking', 'nodding' etc. The child who performs the chosen action might use a hand puppet.

Hickety tickety

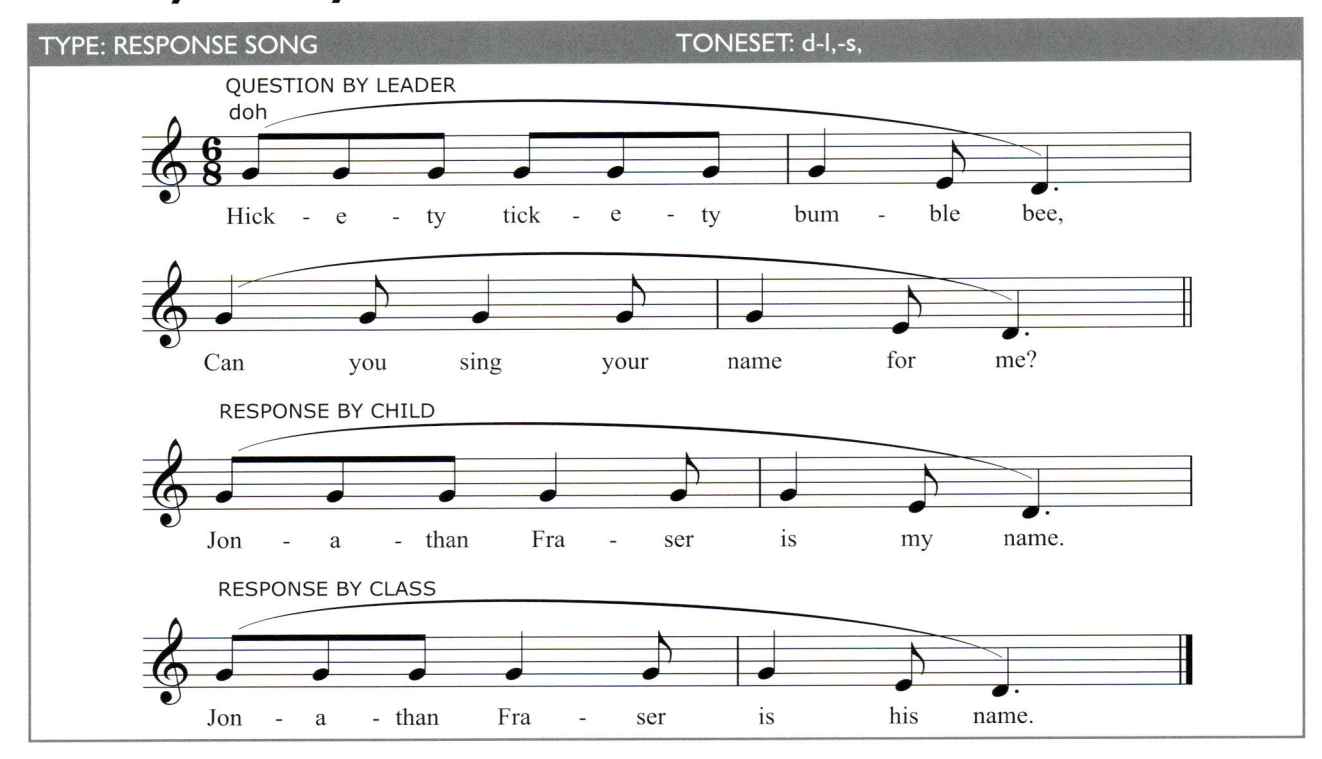

TYPE: RESPONSE SONG **TONESET: d-l,-s,**

QUESTION BY LEADER
doh
Hick - e - ty tick - e - ty bum - ble bee,
Can you sing your name for me?

RESPONSE BY CHILD
Jon - a - than Fra - ser is my name.

RESPONSE BY CLASS
Jon - a - than Fra - ser is his name.

DESCRIPTION OF GAME, ACTION OR ACTIVITY

This song is very useful for helping children in making an individual response. Initially the teacher will be the leader and gently encourage a response from the individual child. A more reticent child may, in the first instance, require some support but will immediately gain in confidence when the class responds with his or her name. It can be helpful and a 'comfort' when a favourite toy such as the class mascot is handed to the child during the leader's question. Some will take heart and grow in confidence when a child takes the role of leader.

How many miles to Babylon?

TYPE: GAME SONG **TONESET:** s-m-r-d

(CHILD 1 + 2) How many miles to Babylon?
(CLASS) Three score and ten.
(CHILD 1 + 2) Will we be there by Candlemas?
(CLASS) Yes and back again.
(CHILD 1 + 2) Open your gates and let us through.
(CLASS) Not without a beck and boo.
(CHILD 1) Here's the beck.
(CHILD 2) Here's the boo.
(CLASS) Open the gates and let them through.

DESCRIPTION OF GAME, ACTION OR ACTIVITY

The children form two lines. The top couple turn and face down towards the other end of their line. They sing the questions and everyone else answers. At "Here's the beck", the first child throws his head and shoulders backwards and at "Here's the boo", the partner drops her head and shoulders forward. The lines form arches and the couple goes under to the other end. The game continues with the new top couple.

I have a dog

TYPE: SONG　　　　　　　　　　　　　　TONESET: s-m-r-d

(me) I have a *dog and *his name is *Ro-ver,
*He is the one I love the best.

2. When *he is good, *he is good all over,
   When *he is bad *he is just a pest.

DESCRIPTION OF GAME, ACTION OR ACTIVITY

* Once the song is well known, encourage children to sing about their own pets or favourite animal toys [eg teddy bear] with appropriate words. In addition, the class could repeat the child's words but substituting "I" with the singer's name and replacing "I love the best" with "that she/he loves best".

I have lost the cupboard key

TYPE: GAME SONG　　　　　　　　　　　TONESET: m-r-d

SOLO (doh)
I have lost the cup-board key some-where in the class-room.

CLASS
We will help you find the key some-where in the class-room.

DESCRIPTION OF GAME, ACTION OR ACTIVITY

A child leaves the room. Another then hides the key. The first child returns and is guided by the class in finding the key, singing the second phrase more quietly when she is far from the key and louder as she gets nearer to it. The song is repeated as often as is necessary for the 'seeker' to find the key or the search is abandoned.

Singing Development: The children are being asked to show vocal control and an ability to sing with variations of dynamic. They are asked not to lose their Singing Voices – that is, to avoid the extremes of whispering or shouting. For this activity it might be better if the class stands.

I, I, me oh my [© 1977 by Boosey & Hawkes Music Publishers Ltd]

TYPE: SONG   **TONESET: s-m**

I, I, me oh my, how I like my ap-ple pie.

2. …How I like my cherry pie.
3. …How I like my shepherd's pie.
4. …How I like my fish pie.

DESCRIPTION OF GAME, ACTION OR ACTIVITY

As the children sing the song, an object representing a pie is passed round a circle. Whoever is holding the pie at the end of the song can choose a pie for the class to sing as a next verse.

As the song becomes known, invite a child to sing her choice of pie (the whole verse) while holding the pie. The class repeats this new verse as the pie is passed round the circle once more to find a new solo singer. The class should imitate the pitch, tempo, dynamics and words of the solo child.

Singing Development: This is a very useful song for building individual confidence and careful listening and imitation by the others.

I see you

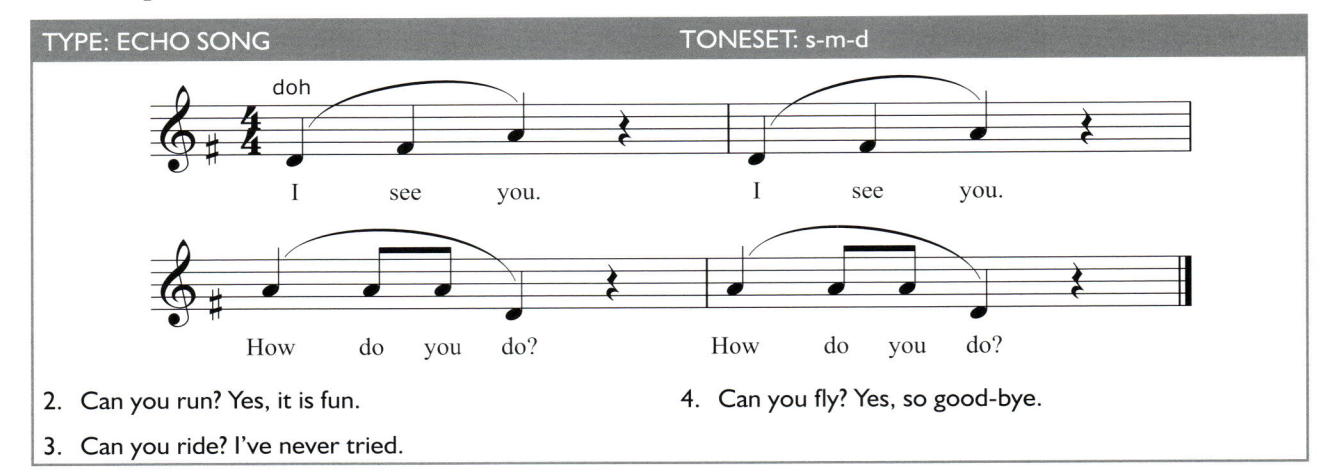

| TYPE: ECHO SONG | TONESET: s-m-d |

(Music notation: doh)
I see you. I see you.
How do you do? How do you do?

2. Can you run? Yes, it is fun.
3. Can you ride? I've never tried.
4. Can you fly? Yes, so good-bye.

DESCRIPTION OF GAME, ACTION OR ACTIVITY

The class echoes each phrase sung by the leader.

Other ways can be easily devised for performing this song so that there is contrast as the singing moves from one phrase to another, for example:

- changes of dynamic level
- changes of tempo
- class echoed by small group or solo child
- voice followed by instrument
- echoes from a distant location

Ask the children to invent new verses.

Ickle, ockle

TYPE: GAME SONG **TONESET: l-s-m-d**

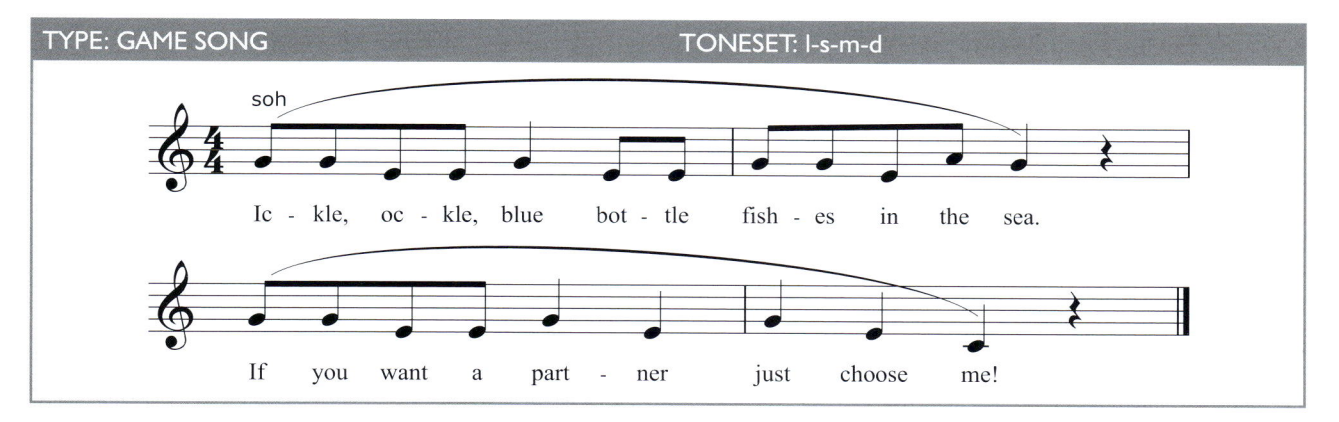

Ickle, ockle, blue bottle fishes in the sea.
If you want a partner just choose me!

DESCRIPTION OF GAME, ACTION OR ACTIVITY

The class forms a circle and a child walks round the inside as the class sings. At the end the child chooses a partner and, as the song is sung again, the pair alternately slap each other's hands and their own knees in time with the pulse. The second child now remains in the centre and the game begins again.

Later, several children might start in the centre of the circle.

Jack in the box

TYPE: ACTION SONG **TONESET: s-m-d**

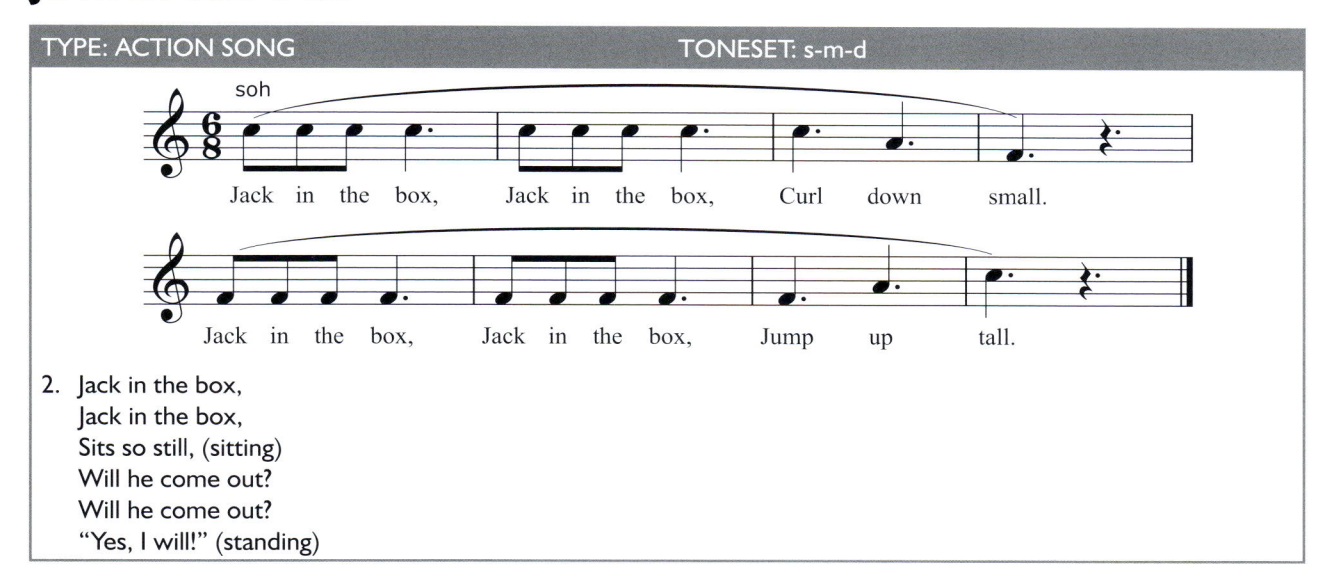

Jack in the box, Jack in the box, Curl down small.
Jack in the box, Jack in the box, Jump up tall.

2. Jack in the box,
   Jack in the box,
   Sits so still, (sitting)
   Will he come out?
   Will he come out?
   "Yes, I will!" (standing)

DESCRIPTION OF GAME, ACTION OR ACTIVITY

When the song is known, the children sing and perform actions as suggested by the words.

A small group sings the song while the others perform the actions of Jack in the box. Alternatively, the children might divide into pairs and take it in turns to be singers or Jack in the box.

Individuals could sing and manipulate a toy Jack in the box or puppet.

Jelly on a plate

TYPE: SKIPPING RHYME **TONESET:** Chant

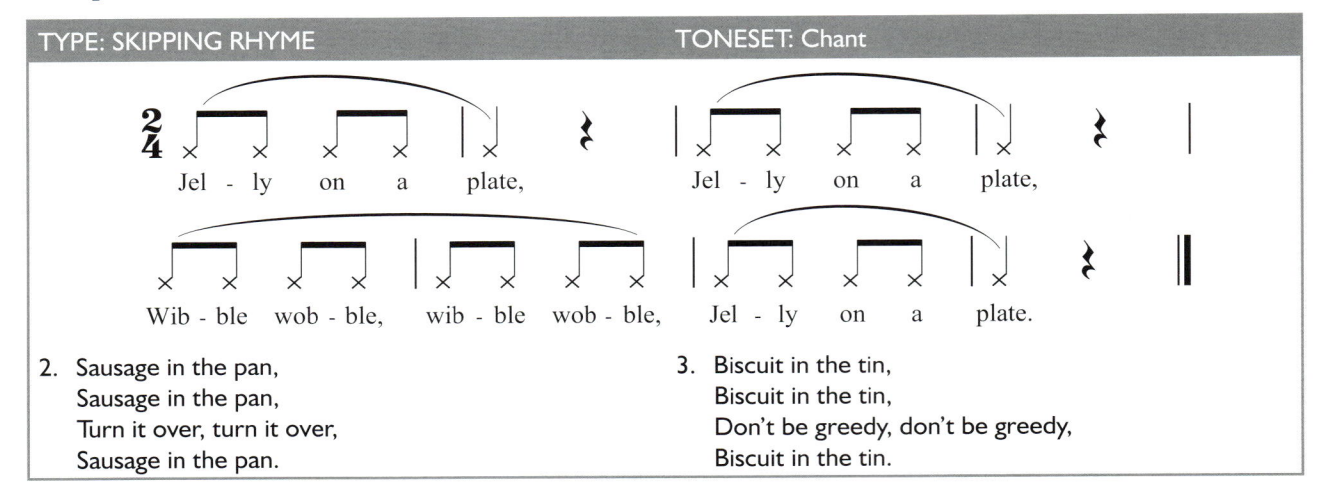

Jel-ly on a plate, Jel-ly on a plate,
Wib-ble wob-ble, wib-ble wob-ble, Jel-ly on a plate.

2. Sausage in the pan,
   Sausage in the pan,
   Turn it over, turn it over,
   Sausage in the pan.

3. Biscuit in the tin,
   Biscuit in the tin,
   Don't be greedy, don't be greedy,
   Biscuit in the tin.

DESCRIPTION OF GAME, ACTION OR ACTIVITY

This is a chant in which children move to the feel of the pulse. For example:

- Verse 1   Jelly   Make wobbly movements with the body.
- Verse 2   Sausage   Make a 'roly-poly' movement with the hands.
- Verse 3   Biscuit   Make a 'scolding' movement with one finger.

Listen, listen, here I come

TYPE: GAME SONG **TONESET:** s-m-r-d

Lis-ten, lis-ten, here I come, Some-one spe-cial gets the drum.

DESCRIPTION OF GAME, ACTION OR ACTIVITY

The children stand in a circle. As the class sings the song, a child performs a steady pulse on a portable drum while walking round inside the circle. At the end of the song the child stops, and the nearest person in the circle now becomes the drummer. The first child takes the new child's place in the circle and the game continues.

Variations:

- The children in the circle are asked to close their eyes during the game.
- The solo child is encouraged to use the Thinking Voice while still playing the drum.
- The drummer is asked to play the rhythm of the song instead of the pulse.

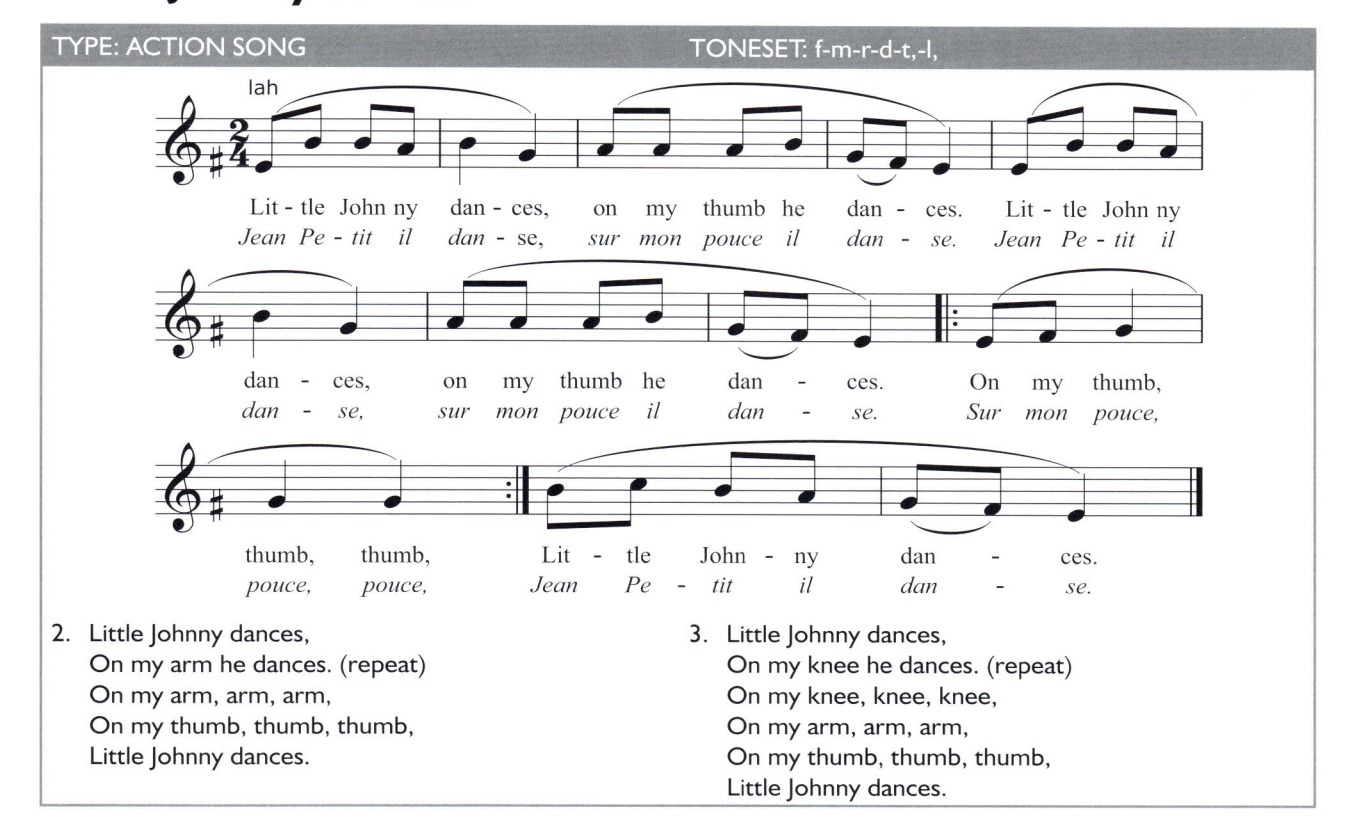

Little Johnny dances

TYPE: ACTION SONG **TONESET: f-m-r-d-t,-l,**

(lah)

Lit-tle John-ny dan-ces, on my thumb he dan-ces. Lit-tle John-ny dan-ces, on my thumb he dan-ces. On my thumb, thumb, thumb, Lit-tle John-ny dan-ces.

Jean Pe-tit il dan-se, sur mon pouce il dan-se. Jean Pe-tit il dan-se, sur mon pouce il dan-se. Sur mon pouce, pouce, pouce, Jean Pe-tit il dan-se.

2. Little Johnny dances,
   On my arm he dances. (repeat)
   On my arm, arm, arm,
   On my thumb, thumb, thumb,
   Little Johnny dances.

3. Little Johnny dances,
   On my knee he dances. (repeat)
   On my knee, knee, knee,
   On my arm, arm, arm,
   On my thumb, thumb, thumb,
   Little Johnny dances.

DESCRIPTION OF GAME, ACTION OR ACTIVITY

This is a cumulative song, allowing any number of dancing points for 'Johnny the puppet' to be added in the way shown. Phrase 5 of the notation is used repeatedly for "On my thumb/arm/knee" etc. Each child can use a 'puppet-hand' to tap the rhythm or the pulse on the relevant part of the body.

A string puppet worked by the teacher or a child could be very effective during the performance of the song to onlookers.

The words in French are very easy for children and could form part of a project to identify parts of the body in French.

French: verse 2 – 'arm' = 'bras'; verse 3 – 'knee' = 'genou'.

Little Sally Saucer

TYPE: GAME SONG **TONESET: l-s-m**

soh

Little Sally Saucer, Sitting in the water.
Rise, Sally, Rise, Now wipe your eyes.
(spoken) Turn to the East, Turn to the West.
Turn to the one that you like best.

DESCRIPTION OF GAME, ACTION OR ACTIVITY

The children form a circle with a chosen child in the middle – 'Sally', or 'Sammy' for boys or, indeed, the child's own name might be used, for example "Little Andy Saucer". The class sings the song and 'Sally' performs according to the words. During the spoken section, the child's eyes are closed and s/he turns round and round with an outstretched pointing finger until the song ends. The child indicated becomes the next 'Sally'.

Published by The Voices Foundation and Alfred Publishing Co
© The Voices Foundation 2014

Lots of rosy apples

TYPE: GAME SONG **TONESET:** s-m-r-d

SOLO: Lots of ro-sy ap-ples on the tree. Pick one for (Ja-son) and one for me.

CLASS: Take a box and fill it up right to the top. When it's flow-ing o-ver it's time to stop.

DESCRIPTION OF GAME, ACTION OR ACTIVITY

A child sings the first two phrases, naming someone in the class in the second phrase. The class sings the rest of the song, during which the first child presents a ball to the named child. Ball in hand, the named child then becomes the new leader and names a new child in the second phrase, as before.

For added fun, one child volunteers to be the 'tree' and stands holding an 'apple' (ball) on each outstretched 'branch' (arm). The solo child picks each 'apple' in turn from each 'branch' as he sings the first two phrases. The 'apple-picker' takes an 'apple' to the named child and retains the other.

Singing Development: It is best if all the children stand to sing this song in order to encourage the correct posture and support for the sudden leap in pitch in the middle of each phrase. It can help children who experience difficulty in raising the pitch of the voice sufficiently to stretch one arm above their heads at that moment as though 'picking an apple high up in the apple tree'.

Mice, mice

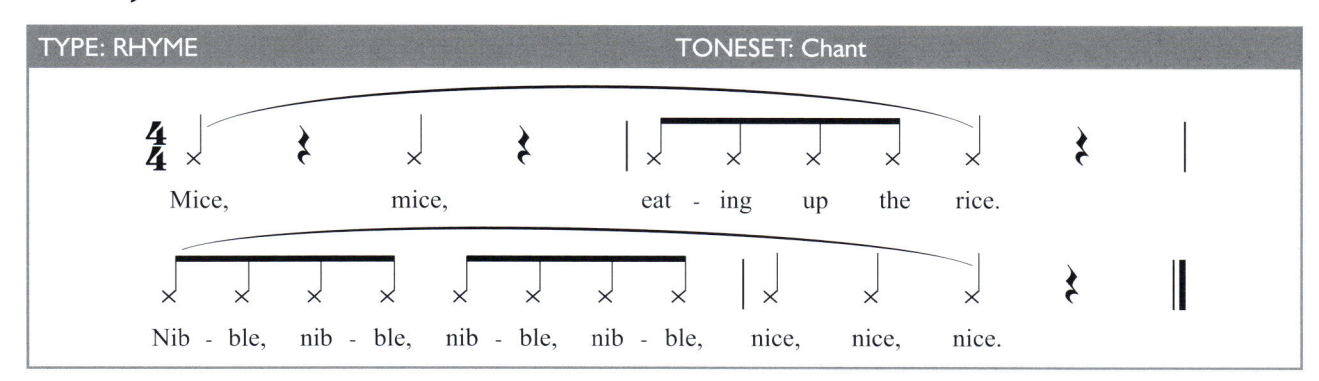

TYPE: RHYME **TONESET:** Chant

Mice, mice, eat-ing up the rice.
Nib-ble, nib-ble, nib-ble, nib-ble, nice, nice, nice.

DESCRIPTION OF GAME, ACTION OR ACTIVITY

The children speak the rhyme with a quiet voice, simultaneously tapping with two fingers the rhythm of the words into the palm of the other hand, suggesting mice nibbling the rice! At each silent rest, the tapping fingers are put to the lips to emphasise 'no sound'. If available, finger puppet mice can add to the fun.

The rhyme can be performed with the children using their Thinking Voices and the rhythm tapped on their hands. One child – or several children – could be invited to perform the rhythm only, on instruments such as claves or woodblocks.

Miss, miss

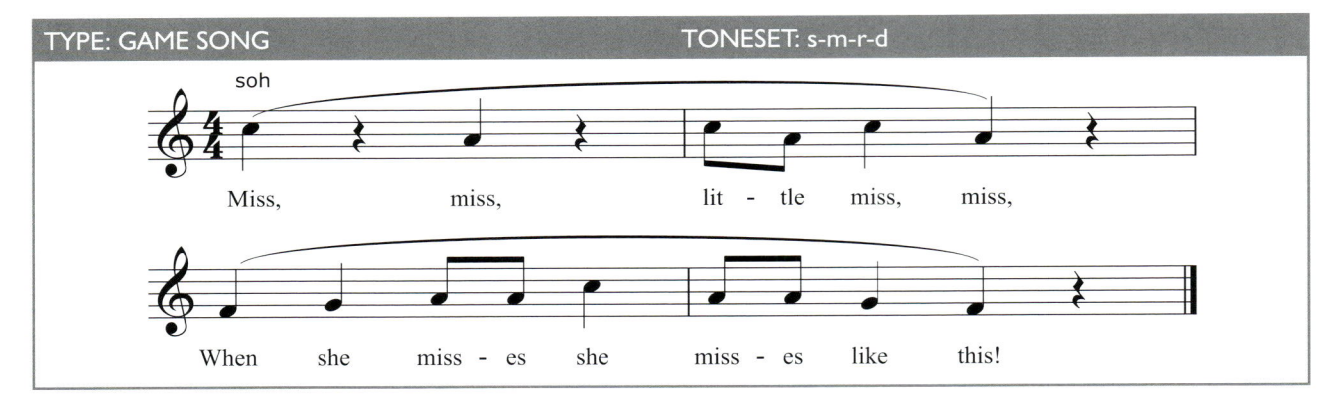

TYPE: GAME SONG **TONESET: s-m-r-d**

Miss, miss, lit-tle miss, miss,
When she miss-es she miss-es like this!

DESCRIPTION OF GAME, ACTION OR ACTIVITY

In pairs each child sings and repeatedly claps own hands, slaps the partner's hands in time to the pulse. Immediately after "this!" both children try to miss slapping the other's hands.

With due care, the pairs could try the actions with closed eyes.

Using the children's game of 'shoot', the pairs carry out the same actions but end with shooting forward one finger or two. Evens, ie two single fingers or two fingers from both children, is a 'hit'. Odds, ie a single from one and two from the other, is a 'miss'.

On a log

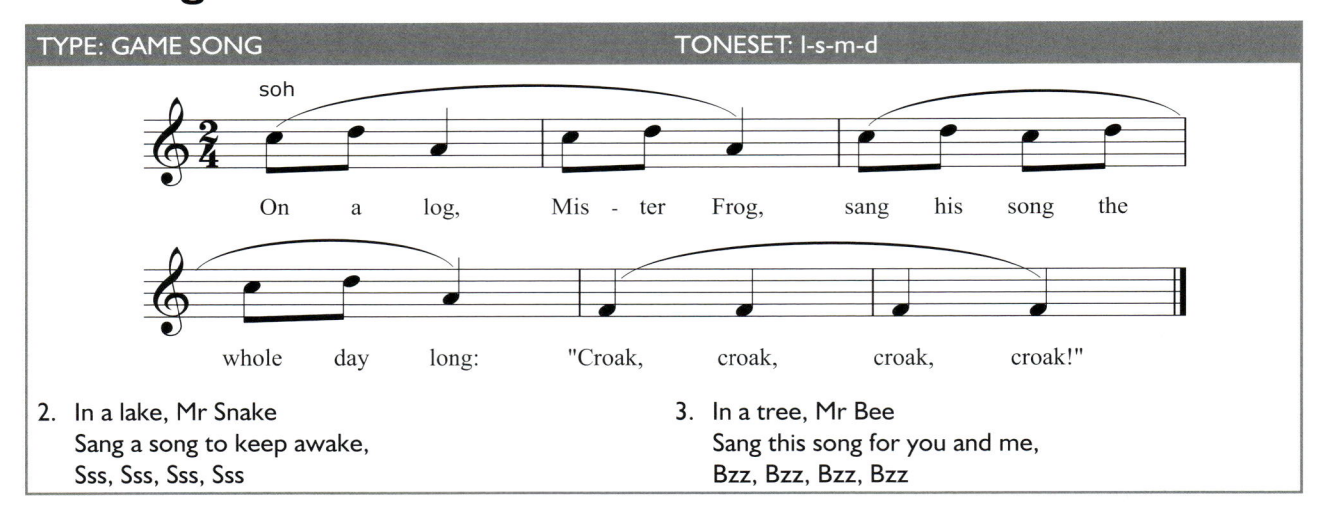

TYPE: GAME SONG **TONESET: l-s-m-d**

On a log, Mis-ter Frog, sang his song the whole day long: "Croak, croak, croak, croak!"

2. In a lake, Mr Snake
   Sang a song to keep awake,
   Sss, Sss, Sss, Sss

3. In a tree, Mr Bee
   Sang this song for you and me,
   Bzz, Bzz, Bzz, Bzz

DESCRIPTION OF GAME, ACTION OR ACTIVITY

The children form a circle, the edge of the pond. In the middle sits Mr Frog. The song is sung. On each "croak" Mr Frog jumps four times to a chosen child in the circle who becomes the next Mr Frog. The child who is Mr Frog might sing the "croaks" by himself as he jumps.

The other verses can be similarly interpreted.

Perhaps other verses could be devised.

Once a man fell in a well

TYPE: SONG TONESET: s-f-m-r-d

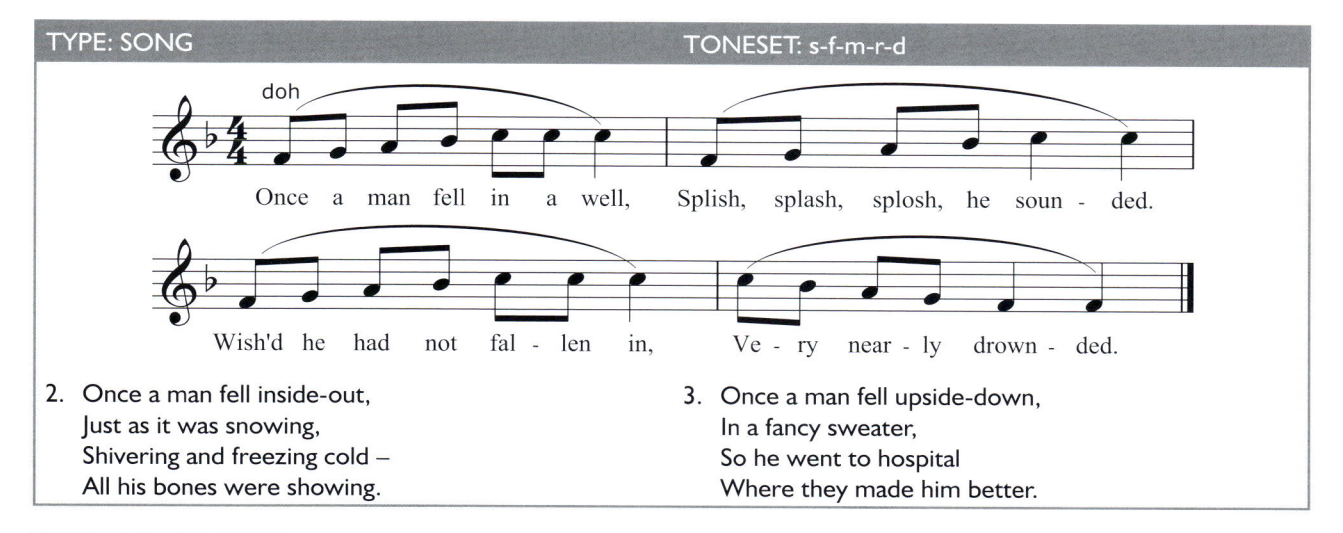

Once a man fell in a well, Splish, splash, splosh, he soun-ded.
Wish'd he had not fal-len in, Ve-ry near-ly drown-ded.

2. Once a man fell inside-out,
   Just as it was snowing,
   Shivering and freezing cold –
   All his bones were showing.

3. Once a man fell upside-down,
   In a fancy sweater,
   So he went to hospital
   Where they made him better.

DESCRIPTION OF GAME, ACTION OR ACTIVITY

After learning to sing the song, ask the children to notice how the pitch of the melody moves by step – ascending three times and descending once. You may be able to illustrate this with drawings, or staging steps, or a staircase construction using materials to hand.

Peter taps with one hammer

TYPE: ACTION SONG TONESET: m-r-d

Pe-ter taps with one ham-mer, one ham-mer, one ham-mer,
Pe-ter taps with one ham-mer all day long.

DESCRIPTION OF GAME, ACTION OR ACTIVITY

The children sit on chairs for this song.
One hammer: children tap with one hand on the thigh to the feel of the pulse.
Two hammers: tap with both hands on each thigh.
Three hammers: tap with both hands and one foot.
Four hammers: tap with both hands and both feet.
Five hammers: tap with both hands and feet and one head!

Pitter, patter

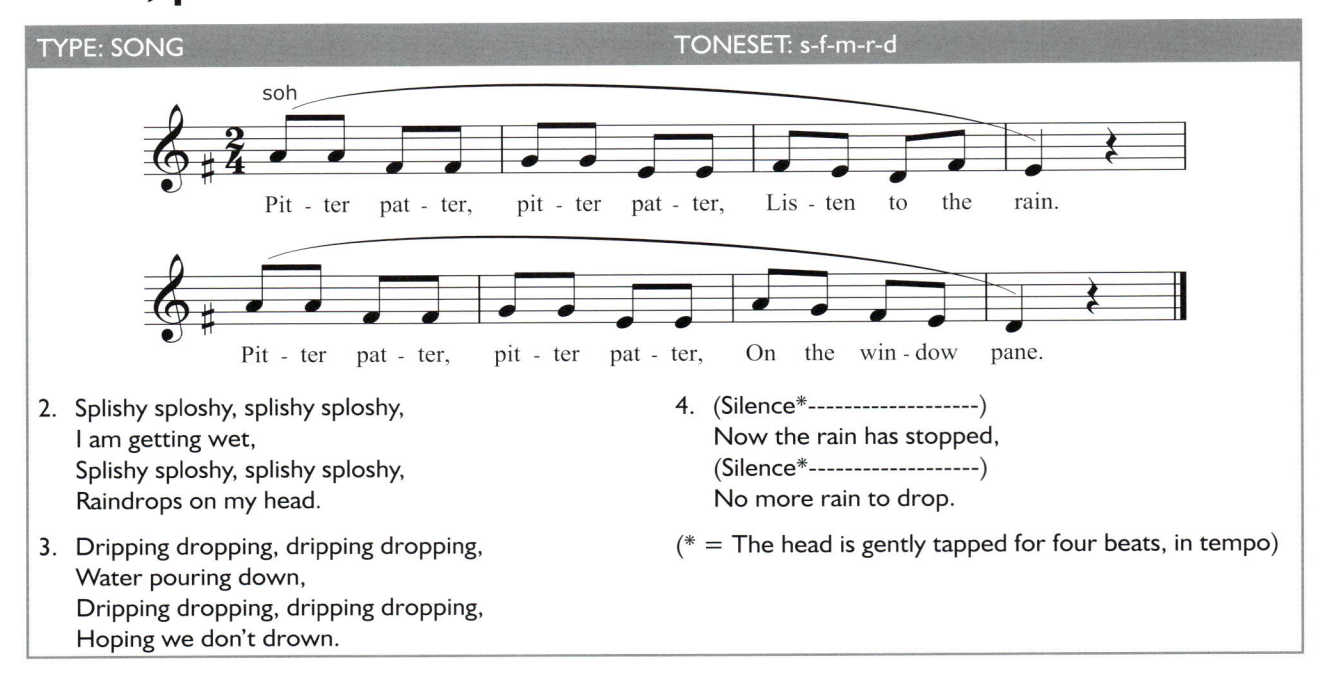

TYPE: SONG   **TONESET: s-f-m-r-d**

soh

Pit-ter pat-ter, pit-ter pat-ter, Lis-ten to the rain.

Pit-ter pat-ter, pit-ter pat-ter, On the win-dow pane.

2. Splishy sploshy, splishy sploshy,
   I am getting wet,
   Splishy sploshy, splishy sploshy,
   Raindrops on my head.

3. Dripping dropping, dripping dropping,
   Water pouring down,
   Dripping dropping, dripping dropping,
   Hoping we don't drown.

4. (Silence*-------------------)
   Now the rain has stopped,
   (Silence*-------------------)
   No more rain to drop.

   (* = The head is gently tapped for four beats, in tempo)

DESCRIPTION OF GAME, ACTION OR ACTIVITY

The children sing and tap the rhythm of each verse. To suggest the incremental force of the rain, one finger taps the rhythm in verse 1, in verse 2 two fingers are used and in verse 3 the whole hand is used. However in verse 4, they gently tap the pulse on their heads for the 'silences' and sing only for the rest.

Instruments might be used instead of hands. Invite children to suggest suitable instruments and to give their reasons. How will the incremental effect of the rain be achieved through a change in dynamics? Consider the effects of adding instruments and how a change in dynamics is obtained by the way in which they are played. Also, be aware of the dynamic balance between voices and instruments.

Published by The Voices Foundation and Alfred Publishing Co
© The Voices Foundation 2014

Rain is falling down

TYPE: SONG **TONESET: m-r-d**

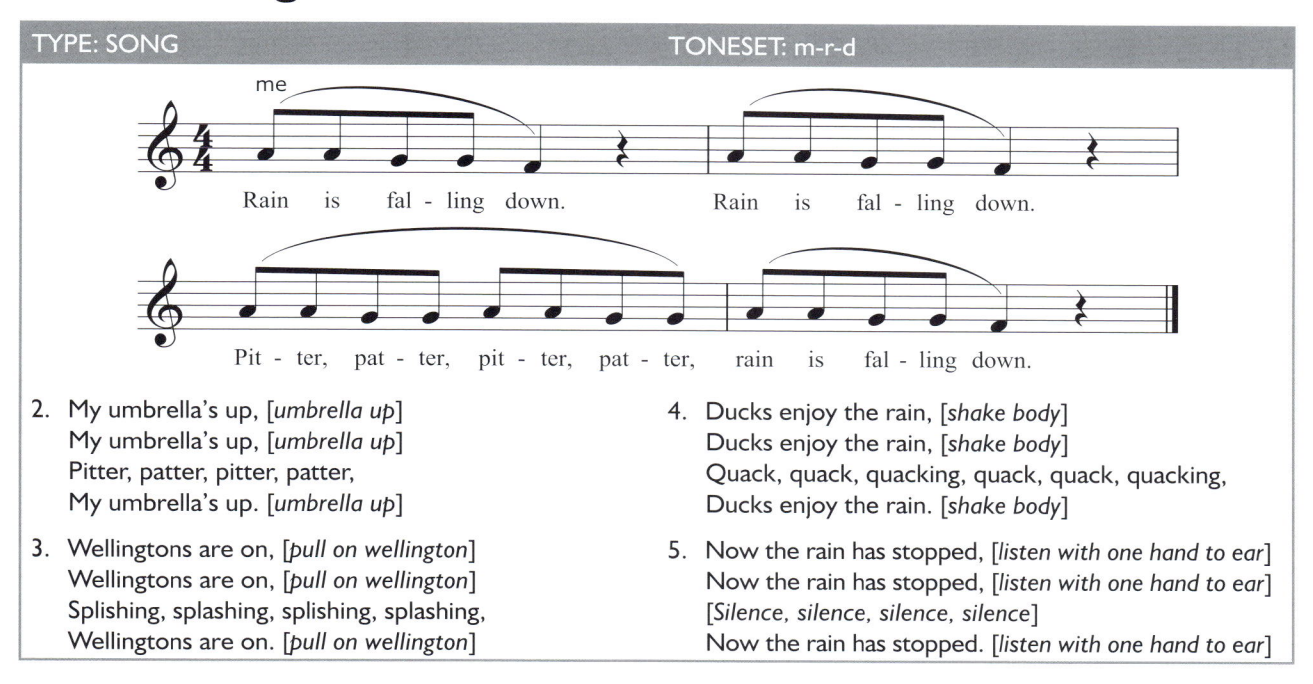

(me) Rain is fal-ling down. Rain is fal-ling down.
Pit-ter, pat-ter, pit-ter, pat-ter, rain is fal-ling down.

2. My umbrella's up, [*umbrella up*]
   My umbrella's up, [*umbrella up*]
   Pitter, patter, pitter, patter,
   My umbrella's up. [*umbrella up*]

3. Wellingtons are on, [*pull on wellington*]
   Wellingtons are on, [*pull on wellington*]
   Splishing, splashing, splishing, splashing,
   Wellingtons are on. [*pull on wellington*]

4. Ducks enjoy the rain, [*shake body*]
   Ducks enjoy the rain, [*shake body*]
   Quack, quack, quacking, quack, quack, quacking,
   Ducks enjoy the rain. [*shake body*]

5. Now the rain has stopped, [*listen with one hand to ear*]
   Now the rain has stopped, [*listen with one hand to ear*]
   [*Silence, silence, silence, silence*]
   Now the rain has stopped. [*listen with one hand to ear*]

DESCRIPTION OF GAME, ACTION OR ACTIVITY

Each of the first four verses has a single, silent action at the end of phrases 1, 2 & 4, in the melodic rest. In verse 5 phrase 3, the children use their Thinking Voices. Verse 1 could have the action of both hands on the head, cowering from the rain.

Rain on the green grass

TYPE: ACTION SONG **TONESET: s-d**

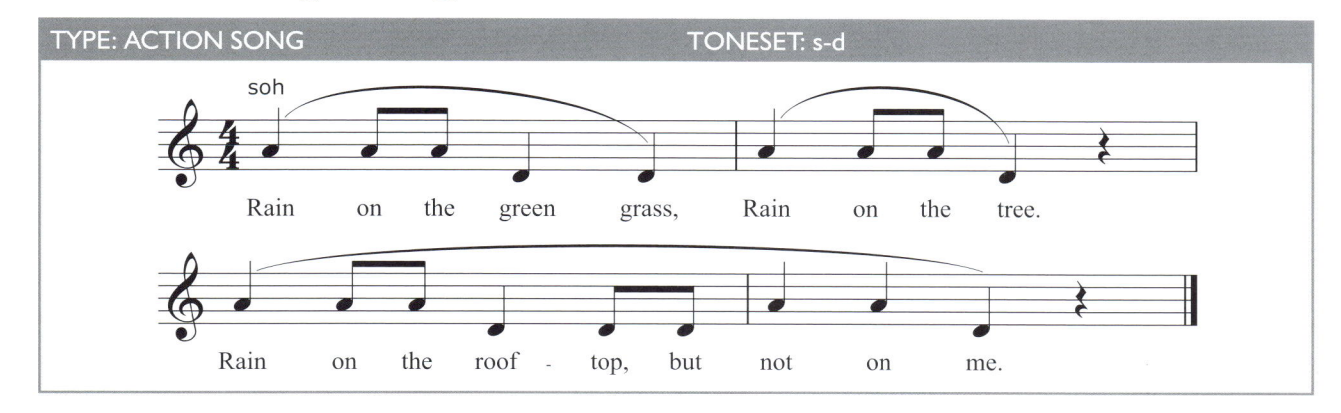

(soh) Rain on the green grass, Rain on the tree.
Rain on the roof-top, but not on me.

DESCRIPTION OF GAME, ACTION OR ACTIVITY

Use fingers to represent the grass, arms for the tree, hands shaped for the roof and for "Not on me", hands on head to cower.

Rain, rain, go away

TYPE: SONG	TONESET: l-s-m

[Musical notation with lyrics: "Rain, rain, go a-way, Come a-gain a-no-ther day."]

2. Which day shall I come?
   Come again on Monday
   (Tuesday, Wednesday …)

3. Sunshine's here to stay,
   Now we can go out to play.

DESCRIPTION OF GAME, ACTION OR ACTIVITY

The class chooses a day of the week and, after singing verse 1, a selected child representing a 'rain cloud', sings phrase 1 of verse 2: "Which day shall I come?" The class replies, using the words, "Come again on Monday, Tuesday, etc … until the agreed day of the week is reached. The last verse is used to bring the song to an end.

Round and round the village

TYPE: GAME SONG	TONESET: d'-t-l-s-f-m-r-d-t,

[Musical notation with lyrics: "Round and round the vil-lage, Round and round the vil-lage, Round and round the vil-lage, As we have done be-fore."]

2. In and out the windows,
   In and out the windows,
   In and out the windows,
   As we have done before.

3. Stand and face your partner, *etc.*

4. Shake hands with your partner, *etc.*

DESCRIPTION OF GAME, ACTION OR ACTIVITY

Verse 1: One child skips round the outside of the circle formed with joined hands.

Verse 2: He then skips in and out under their raised arms.

Verse 3: He stands in front of his chosen partner.

Verse 4: He shakes hands with his partner and they exchange places, ready for the partner to restart the game.

Sally go round the sun

TYPE: ACTION SONG **TONESET: l-s-m-r-d**

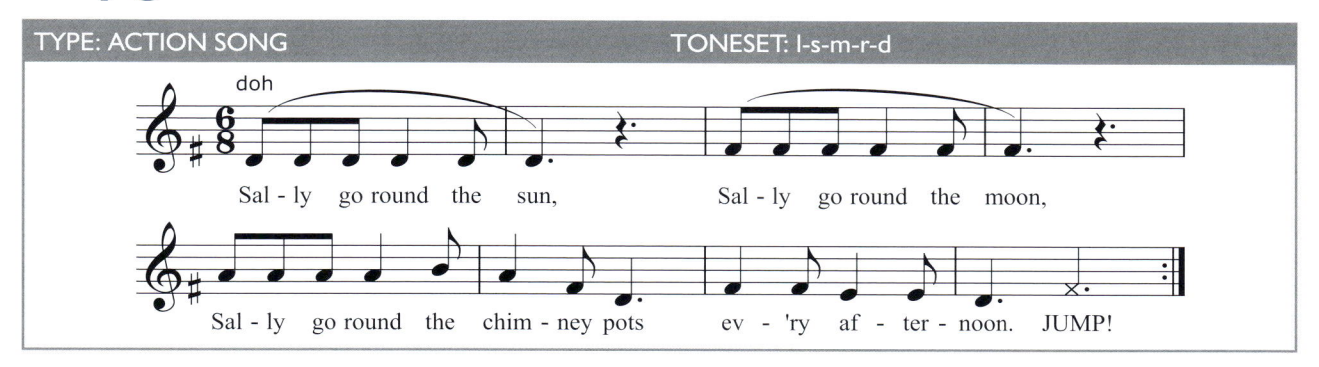

Sal - ly go round the sun, Sal - ly go round the moon, Sal - ly go round the chim - ney pots ev - 'ry af - ter - noon. JUMP!

DESCRIPTION OF GAME, ACTION OR ACTIVITY

The children join hands as a circle and dance round in one direction. At "JUMP!" they stop and jump. The song is repeated, with the circle moving in the opposite direction and with a jump at the end. The days of the week can be used in the last phrase, eg "… on a Sunday afternoon." Each repeat could change the day of the week. Where space is limited, it is often better and safer for there to be a number of circles singing simultaneously or performing consecutively.

Snail, snail

TYPE: ACTION SONG **TONESET: l-s-m**

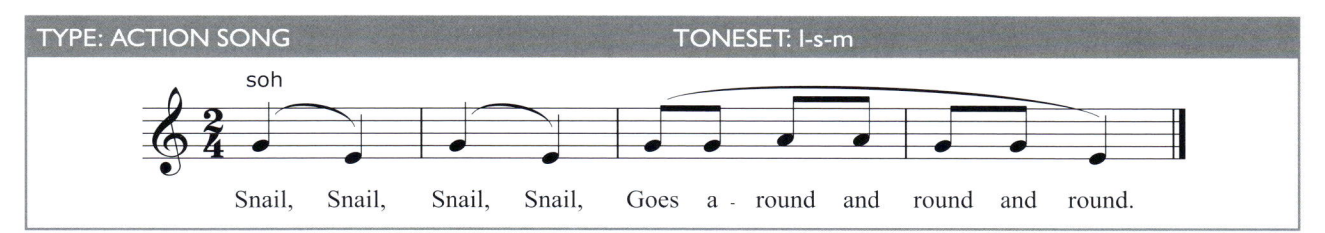

Snail, Snail, Snail, Snail, Goes a - round and round and round.

DESCRIPTION OF GAME, ACTION OR ACTIVITY

The class forms a circle. Singing the song, the children walk round in a circle in time to the pulse, noting how slow their steps need to be because there is nothing speedy about a snail. The aim is to achieve the slow tempo with accuracy.

As an alternative, it may be prudent to form several smaller circles of fewer numbers. Having had time to practise, each circle performs the song and the movement. Draw the attention of the whole class to any circle that performs with accuracy.

Spinning top

| TYPE: SONG | TONESET: s-m-d |

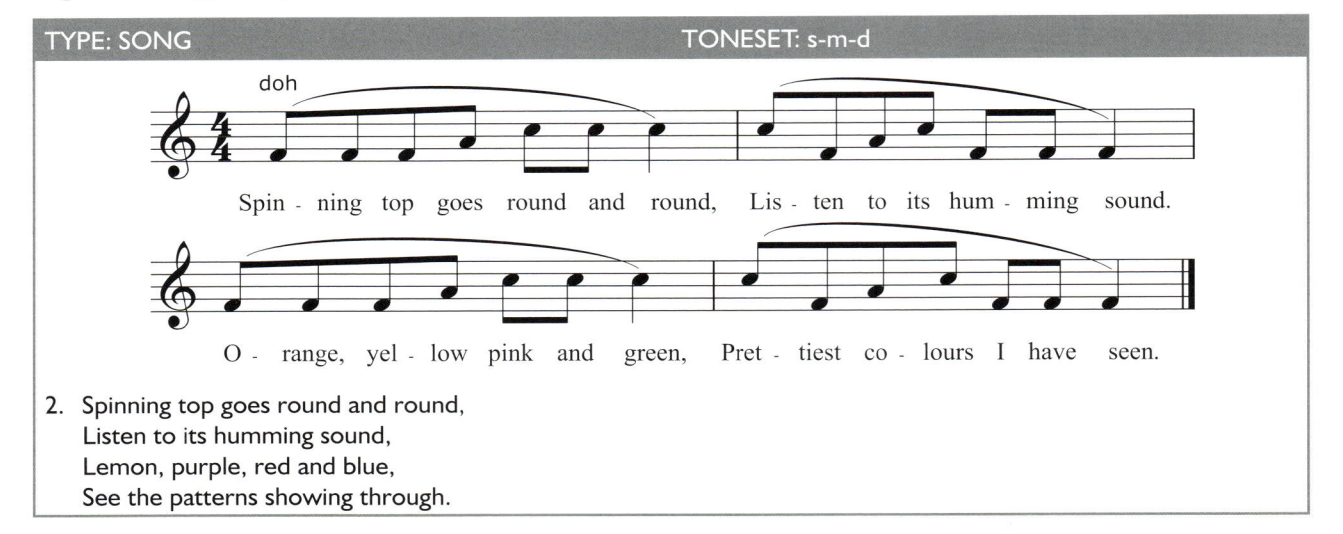

[Musical notation with lyrics:]
Spin-ning top goes round and round, Lis-ten to its hum-ming sound.
O-range, yel-low pink and green, Pret-tiest co-lours I have seen.

2. Spinning top goes round and round,
   Listen to its humming sound,
   Lemon, purple, red and blue,
   See the patterns showing through.

DESCRIPTION OF GAME, ACTION OR ACTIVITY

All the children sing the song through and then hum the melody through once.

The children are divided into two groups. Group A sings with words of verse 1, followed immediately by Group B humming the melody. Group B then sings verse 2, followed by Group A humming. Finally, Group A sings the first verse once more as Group B simultaneously hums the melody.

A humming top is set in motion and the song is sung to accompany it.

Starlight, star bright

| TYPE: SONG | TONESET: l-s-m-r-d |

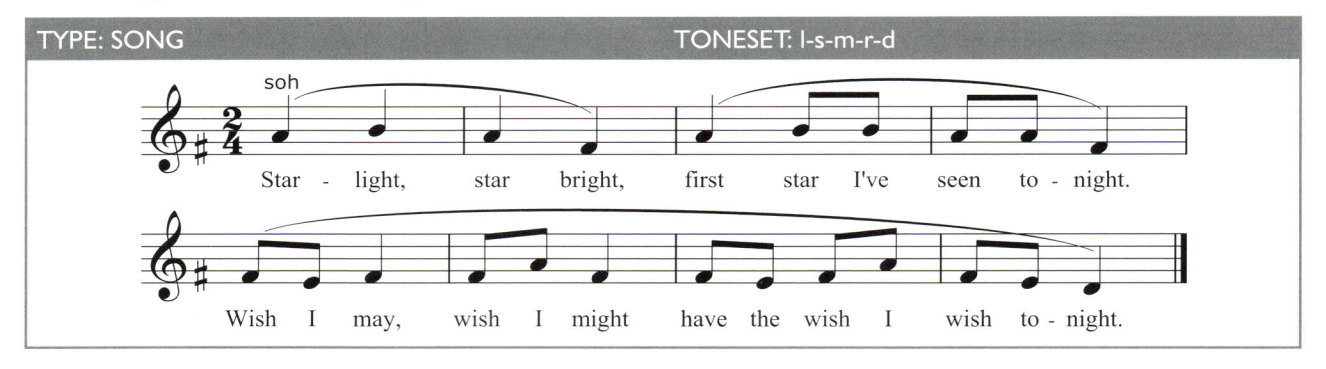

[Musical notation with lyrics:]
Star-light, star bright, first star I've seen to-night.
Wish I may, wish I might have the wish I wish to-night.

DESCRIPTION OF GAME, ACTION OR ACTIVITY

The words are those of a traditional wishing rhyme, probably said by children in the past as they got into bed for the night.

The children kneel in a circle, with one child holding a comfortably large ball. During the singing of the song the ball is passed in time to the pulse, and whoever holds the ball on the last sound is encouraged to make a secret wish. A 'wisher' may choose to share her wish with everyone.

Suo gân

TYPE: SONG **TONESET: m-r-d**

Su - o gân, do not weep. Su - o gân, go to sleep.
Su - o gân, have no fear. Su - o gân, Mother's near.

DESCRIPTION OF GAME, ACTION OR ACTIVITY

The word 'suo gân' [pronounced 'see-o gahn'] is a composite Welsh word meaning 'lullaby'.

Singing Challenge: Best sung standing. Ask the children to sing gently and with a smooth swaying feel. They should try to make one singing sound connect to another, rather like beads close together on a thread; this is called 'legato singing'.

There was a man

TYPE: SONG **TONESET: l-s-m-r-d-t,**

There_ was a man lived in the moon, lived in the moon, lived in the moon, there was a man lived in the moon and his name was Aik-en Drum. And he played u-pon a lad-le, a lad-le, a lad-le, and he played up-on a lad-le and his name was Aik-en Drum.

2. His hat was made of good cream cheese, *etc.*
3. His coat was made of good roast beef, *etc.*
4. His buttons were made of penny loaves, *etc.*
5. His waistcoat was made of crust of pies, *etc.*
6. His breeches were made of haggis bags, *etc.*

DESCRIPTION OF GAME, ACTION OR ACTIVITY
Perhaps the children would like to 'dress' the man in the moon with clothes made of different foods.

Three little birds

TYPE: RHYME **TONESET: Chant**

1. Three little birds all fast asleep,
   One little bird said, "Cheep, cheep, cheep"
   Down came Mummy with a big fat crumb
   And the first little bird said, "Yum, yum, yum"

2. Two little birds both fast asleep,
   One little bird said, "Cheep, cheep, cheep"
   Down came Mummy with a big fat crumb
   And the second little bird said, "Yum, yum, yum"

3. One little bird still fast asleep,
   One little bird said, "Cheep, cheep, cheep"
   Down came Mummy with a big fat crumb
   And the third little bird said, "Yum, yum, yum"

DESCRIPTION OF GAME, ACTION OR ACTIVITY
With one of their hands, the children hide their thumb and smallest finger and show the other three fingers curled up. At "One little bird said cheep, cheep, cheep", one of the fingers stands up. During "Down came Mummy", the other hand makes a bird-shape that comes to feed the first little bird.

Tick, tock, see our clock

TYPE: SONG **TONESET: l-s-m-d**

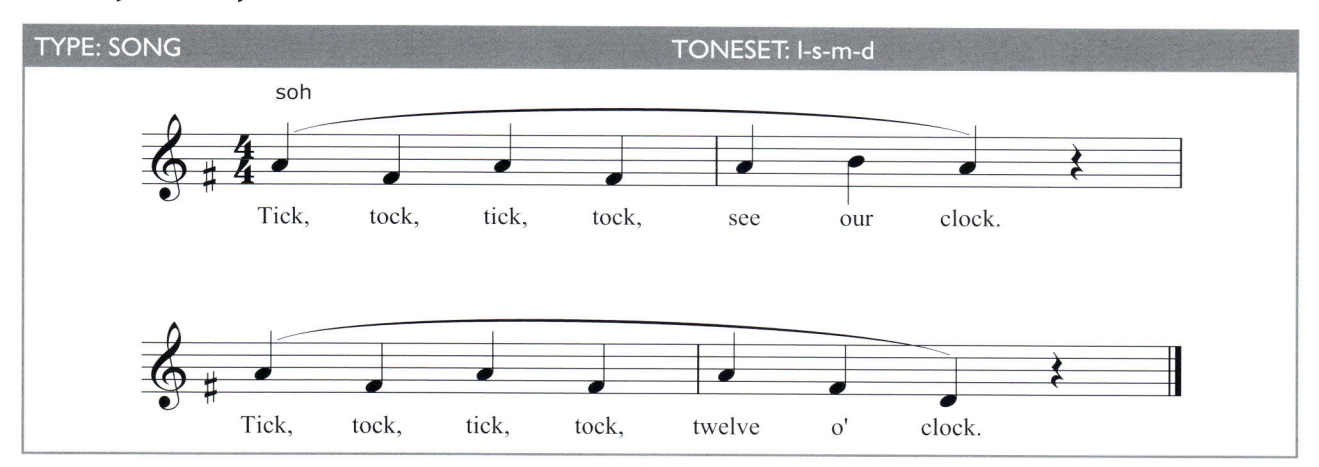

(soh)
Tick, tock, tick, tock, see our clock.
Tick, tock, tick, tock, twelve o' clock.

DESCRIPTION OF GAME, ACTION OR ACTIVITY

Here are two suggested ways to perform this song:

- A teaching clock might be used to show the time about which the children are singing.
- Using a bell-sounding instrument, one child performs a number of chimes, between 1 and 12. The children count the chimes and then use that number as they sing the song.

Touch your shoulders

TYPE: ACTION SONG **TONESET: s-m**

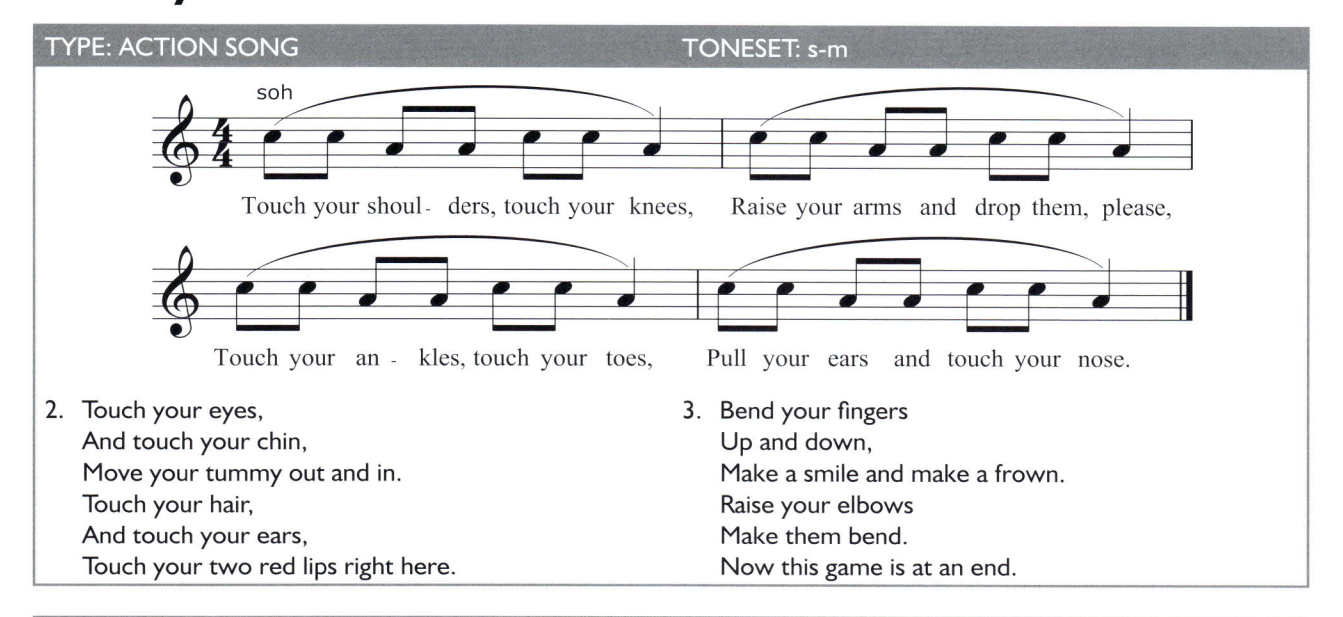

(soh)
Touch your shoul-ders, touch your knees, Raise your arms and drop them, please,
Touch your an-kles, touch your toes, Pull your ears and touch your nose.

2. Touch your eyes,
   And touch your chin,
   Move your tummy out and in.
   Touch your hair,
   And touch your ears,
   Touch your two red lips right here.

3. Bend your fingers
   Up and down,
   Make a smile and make a frown.
   Raise your elbows
   Make them bend.
   Now this game is at an end.

DESCRIPTION OF GAME, ACTION OR ACTIVITY

The actions should move to the pulse, using both hands.

The song could be performed in the following ways:

- Singing without actions
- With actions and the Thinking Voice only

Who has the penny?

TYPE: GAME SONG **TONESET: s-m-r**

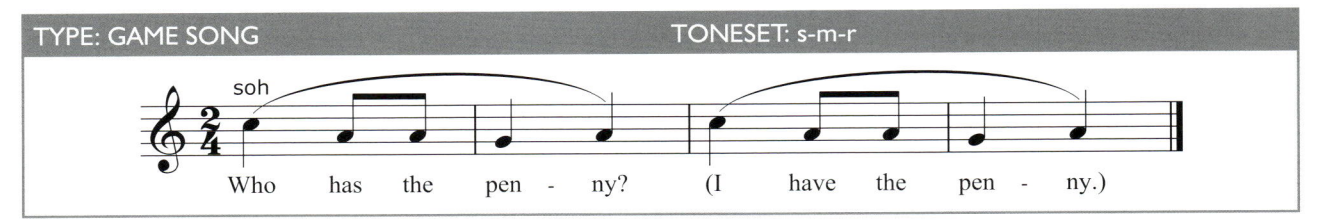

[Musical notation in 2/4, starting on "soh"]

Who has the pen-ny? (I have the pen-ny.)

DESCRIPTION OF GAME, ACTION OR ACTIVITY

The children stand in a circle with outstretched hands. One child sits in the centre of the circle, with eyes closed. Using two or three small common objects previously agreed upon with the class (such as a coin or a key), another child chooses outstretched hands from the circle in which she places each of the objects, while naming them for all to hear. The child in the centre, still with closed eyes, now sings the question "Who has the …?" to his own improvised melody. The child who has the object repeats the melody, using the words "I have the …". The child in the centre identifies this person from the sound of his/her Singing Voice. The game continues in the same way until all the objects are retrieved.

Willum he had seven sons

TYPE: SONG **TONESET: f-m-r-d-t,-l,**

[Musical notation in 4/4, starting on "lah"]

Wil-lum, he had se-ven sons, se-ven sons, se-ven sons,
Wil-lum he had se-ven sons and this is what they did.

2. First they went to fly a plane, fly a plane, fly a plane,
   First they went to fly a plane,
   And this is what they did.

3. Then they went to climb a hill …

4. Then they went to build a wall …

5. Then they went to clean their rooms …

DESCRIPTION OF GAME, ACTION OR ACTIVITY

Ask the children to devise more verses for this song, with each verse having an appropriate accompanying action.

Teaching Extras

Added Bonus Time

At the drop of a hat!

- Things for you and the children to do at odd moments.
- They are listed in an order that corresponds with the progression of the Units.

1. Sing the register, asking the children to respond with their Singing Voices.
2. Make up morning greetings and goodbye response-songs.
3. Encourage the children to sing a current song to a parent or other relative.
4. Encourage the children to teach a well-known song to a parent, sibling or other relative.
5. Sing a song to a partner.
6. Make the lowest [highest, loudest, quietest] sound you can.
7. Make a list of 'sound' words: draw a picture for a 'sound' word.
8. Bring an interesting sound to school.
9. Devise musical signals for instructions, eg to sit, to stand.
10. Sing classroom organisation instructions.
11. Sing a question to individuals, who should then sing their answers.
12. Play 'Who has …?' and 'Who likes …?': the teacher or child sings a question to the class, eg 'Who has a brother?'; using the made-up tune again, the answer comes back: 'I have a brother'; or, again, 'Who likes apples?' 'I like apples'.
13. When things are stressful, stand everyone and sing a gentle song, eg Suo gân, three times: quietly sing / use Thinking Voices / quietly again.
14. Tap the rhythm of a song; ask a partner to identify the song.
15. 'Rhythm of the Day' [use from Unit 16]: a rhythmic phrase from a known song can be displayed, and then before the end of school, the class meet with their answer and sing the relevant song.
16. Where appropriate, work known songs into a story line.
17. When the puppet pops up, the children sing with 'real' sound; when the puppet disappears, the children sing with Thinking Voices.
18. "Apples, peaches, pears and plums, tell me when your birthday comes. January, February, March …": children stand when their month is mentioned; if appropriate, the chant proceeds to numbers, the days of the month; children sit when their number is called.

And you can add in others which occur to you or the children as time goes on ….

Take a Dip!

- This requires two bags such as shoe-bags or similar. One is to hold cards with the titles and/or drawings of the songs that have been learned, the other holds cards with examples of skills acquired from the Units.
- Both bags start empty and gradually fill as more and more songs and skills are learned.
- At certain times when the class or a group is collected together, two children are offered the chance to dip into the bags drawing one activity card and one song card. Always draw an activity card FIRST and read it, followed by a song card. So, for example, the activity card might read 'Tap the rhythm as you sing' AND THEN the song card which might read 'Engine, engine'. The class then proceeds to perform the song and the activity simultaneously. Some combinations will need other groupings or individuals to perform. If you feel the combination presents difficulties, choose a new song or activity card.
- Examples of activities resulting from the skills acquired are given below. You may wish to devise other activities from the children's acquired skills.
- Only the activity title need be written on the card. You can interpret the title from the instructions in the following list.
- An activity does not become available until the relevant Unit has been taught.

What is my song?

Without divulging the title, the child hums the melody of the selected song for the class to recognise.
[from Unit 5]

Sing then think

Class sings the first phrase of the selected song, then repeats the phrase using the Thinking Voice as you tap a steady heartbeat.
[from Unit 7]

Who sang that?

Two or three children take the selected song where they can be heard and not seen. One child sings the song – but which one?
[from Unit 9]

Sing with best voices

Children sing the selected song with best voices to another class/teacher/visitor, or are recorded.
[from Unit 10]

Tap the song

Children tap the rhythm of the selected song as they sing it.
[from Unit 12]

Rainbow phrase

The selected song is sung and each phrase shown by moving the arm in a 'rainbow' arc.
[from Unit 13]

How loud?

Sing the selected song twice, each with a different dynamic, eg very quietly/louder.
[from Unit 14]

Sing – think – sing

Perform the selected song alternating between phrases that are sung ['real' sound] and Thinking Voices ['thinking' sound].
[from Unit 15]

Tap and say ta or teh-teh

Tap and say the rhythm names of a phrase from the selected song BUT only if it uses ta and teh-teh rhythms.
[from Unit 16]

Rhythm and pulse

Walk the pulse and tap the rhythm of the selected song as you sing.
[from Unit 20]

Which song am I?

For this you must first draw two more song titles from the song bag; tap the rhythm of an unannounced song from the short list – which song has that rhythm?
[from Unit 21]

Rhythm burger 1

Sing the selected song; then a child taps a 4-beat rhythm on an instrument using ta and teh-teh rhythms only; repeat the song.
[from Unit 22]

Same or different?

Two groups sing alternate phrases of the selected song and compare them as same or different.
[from Unit 23]

Tempo

Sing the selected song three times at different speeds, eg quicker, slower and very slow tempos.
[from Unit 25]

Dynamics

Sing the selected song three times at different volumes, eg louder, quieter and very quiet dynamics.
[from Unit 25]

New pitch

Three children in turn start the song at a different pitch with "Off you go!"
[from Unit 26]

Lah-soh-me burger

ONLY if the selected song features s-m or l-s-m; after the class has sung the song through, a child signs an improvised singing-names phrase [starting on soh] for the class to sing; the song is then repeated.
[from Unit 28]

Rhythm burger 2

Class sings the selected song through; a child then taps a 4-beat rhythm phrase on an instrument using ta and teh-teh and rest only; the song is then repeated.
[from Unit 29]

Listening Material

Many of the following items are to be found in videos on YouTube. While there are recordings that leave a lot to be desired, some are of sufficient quality in sound and vision to be worth showing to children. When suitable examples are found they will be informative and helpful to the children's understanding of the pieces and widen their knowledge about instruments and their players.

THE GRASSHOPPER'S DANCE — TRACK 62

Composer	Ernest Bucalossi
Performer	The Palm Court Theatre Orchestra /Godwin
Time	3'50"
Source	Chandos

This chirpy piece, dating from 1905, is the best known of the many light music compositions that Bucalossi wrote. The percussion have a field-day producing the sound of the grasshopper, mainly through those instruments made of wood including the xylophone. Is this music to inspire a dance project with the children?

LE COUCOU — TRACK 63

Composer	Louis-Claude Daquin
Performer	Martin Souter
Time	2'13"
Source	The Gift of Music label

Daquin was a much respected keyboard player and organist in France during the 18th century. This lively cameo of the cuckoo's call was part of a suite of short pieces written in 1735. Can the children spot all the characteristic calls?

YouTube: look for a harpsichord upload.

CLOG DANCE — TRACK 64

Composer	Peter Hertel/Lanchbery
Performer	Royal Opera House Orchestra/Lanchbery
Time	2'11"
Source	Decca

This music was incorporated into the ever-popular 1960 ballet La fille mal gardée [The wayward daughter], choreographed by Sir Frederick Ashton. Lise, the daughter of the Widow Simone, tempts her mother with a pair of wooden clogs. Simone performs a hilarious dance in them, attempting, among other things, to 'stand on points'.

YouTube: look out for a video of The Royal Ballet performing this scene – wonderful fun for the children!

IN THE HALL OF THE MOUNTAIN KING		TRACK 65
Composer		Edvard Grieg
Performer		Malmö Symphony Orchestra/Engeset
Time		2'40"
Source		Naxos

The piece forms part of the incidental music written for Ibsen's play, Peer Gynt, in 1876. In a dream-like fantasy, Peer Gynt enters the great hall of the Mountain King: "There is a great crowd of troll courtiers, gnomes and goblins. The Old Man sits on his throne, with crown and sceptre, surrounded by his children and relatives. Peer Gynt stands before him. There is a tremendous uproar in the hall."

YouTube: you may be able to find a video recording of a 'live' performance, useful for seeing how some orchestral instruments are played.

LA TOUPIE		TRACK 66
Composer		Georges Bizet
Performer		Katia and Marielle Labèque
Time		1'01"
Source		Decca/Universal

'La Toupie' [The Top] is one of twelve pieces collectively titled Jeux d'enfants [Children's Games], composed in 1871. The top is a wooden one, spun with the help of a stick and leather cord attached. The great challenge was to set the top in motion and then maintain its spin with the aid of the stick and cord. The music at one point suggests the top is near to 'collapsing', but is whipped to restore the spin.

YouTube: a recording of two pianists at the one piano will give a great idea about the speed at which the fingers need to move in order to create the impression of a fast spinning top.

THE VIENNESE MUSICAL CLOCK		TRACK 67
Composer		Zoltán Kodály
Performer		London Philharmonic Orchestra/Solti
Time		2'06"
Source		Naxos

Kodály is a much-respected composer and philosopher of music education. His opera, Háry János, concerns an old man recounting to tavern listeners exaggerated accounts of his exploits as a brave young soldier. One such tale is how Háry rescued the Emperor of Austria's daughter from the Russians and brought her back to Vienna where everything was strange and fantastic. The most marvellous thing that he saw there was a huge clock. When it chimed the hour, doors opened and a procession of clockwork soldiers emerged to marching music.

YouTube: a video of orchestral players, including the playing of the tubular bells, would provide the children with lots of visual information as they listen.

NUN, GIMEL, HEI, SHIN	TRACK 68
Composer	Judith Shatin
Performer	New London Children's Choir/Corp
Time	2'15"
Source	Naxos

Among the customs of the Jewish festival of Hanukkah are the games for children, being in part instructive and part sheer good fun. On the dreidl, a spinning top, are the initial letters of 'nes gadol haya sham' [a great miracle happened here], in phonetic Hebrew, 'nun, gimel, hei, shin'. The phrase refers to the miracle of the oil lamp within the restored Temple of Jerusalem many centuries ago. This piece reflects the gathering momentum of the dreidl with voices singing in a round, and a solo voice referring to the flat cakes cooked in oil at the time of the festival.

OLIVER CROMWELL	TRACK 69
Composer	Benjamin Britten
Performer	Philip Langridge/Johnson
Time	0'45"
Source	Naxos

This rhyme has its origins in 17th-century Suffolk. It is a piece of blatant satire at Cromwell's expense and, like other so-called nursery rhymes, started life as a piece of adult political humour.

ENTRY OF THE GLADIATORS	TRACK 70
Composer	Julius Fučík
Performer	Band of the Royal Swedish Air Force/Johansson
Time	2'59"
Source	Naxos

Sometimes known as 'Thunder and Blazes', this piece was written by the leading Bohemian bandmaster and martial composer who died in 1916. He wrote numerous marches and many are still part of the marching band repertoire. This, one of the most popular, is now widely associated with the entrance of clowns in a circus performance.

THE ARRIVAL OF THE QUEEN OF SHEBA	TRACK 71
Composer	George Frideric Handel
Performer	Frankfurt Baroque Orchestra/Martini
Time	3'06"
Source	Naxos

In 1749 Handel completed a major composition based on the Biblical account of the visit by the Queen of Sheba to the Israelite court of King Solomon. This piece has often been used by brides for their own entrance music at the start of the marriage ceremony.

YouTube: there will be several videos of reasonable quality for children to see instruments being played.

PARADE	TRACK 72
Composer	Jacques Ibert
Performer	Lamoureux Concerts Orchestra/Sado
Time	2'00"
Source	Naxos

'Parade' is one of a group of pieces that Ibert selected from his music for the play, The Italian Straw Hat, and collectively called them Divertissement (1930). The listener is placed in one spot and witnesses a parade with marching band approach, pass by and recede down the road.

BYDŁO	TRACK 73
Composer	Modest Mussorgsky
Performer	Ukraine National Orchestra/Kuchar
Time	3'17"
Source	Naxos

The composer asks the listener to walk through a picture gallery and stop to contemplate certain paintings that take his fancy. The picture of a 'bydło' is one of a heavy, lumbering ox cart. The suggestion is that the cart is passing the observer and eventually recedes into the distance. 'Bydło' is one of a series of 'pictures' that Mussorgsky wrote as Pictures at an Exhibition in 1874.

YouTube: look for a version that features an orchestra, and let the children enjoy watching the musicians, especially the tuba player.

THE FLIGHT OF THE BUMBLE BEE	TRACK 74
Composer	Nikolay Rimsky-Korsakov
Performer	CSR Symphony Orchestra/Bramhall
Time	1'34"
Source	Naxos

This piece closes Act III of the opera, The Tale of Tsar Saltan (1900), during which the magic Song-Bird changes the Tsar's son into an insect so that he can fly away to visit his father.

YouTube: there are several videos of arrangements for solo instruments, well worth watching for stunning virtuoso performances. Among them you may find the pianist, Yuja Wang.

THE TYPEWRITER	TRACK 75
Composer	Leroy Anderson
Performer	BBC Concert Orchestra/Slatkin
Time	1'43"
Source	Naxos

The composer wrote many light-music classics during the mid-1900s, including 'Sleigh Ride', 'Syncopated Clock', 'Bugler's Holiday' and 'Blue Tango', all with instant appeal but his clever writing gave them timeless appeal, too.

YouTube: among the various uploads is one featuring the percussionist, Martin Breinschmid, performing on an actual typewriter – great fun to see and hear!

O POLICHINELO	TRACK 76
Composer	Heitor Villa-Lobos
Performer	Sonia Rubinsky
Time	0'52"
Source	Naxos

This is one of a group of pieces written under the title Prole do Bebê [Baby's Toys], by probably the most significant figure in 20th-century Brazilian art music. Here we have a lively portrayal of the impish behaviour of someone British children know as Mr Punch.

YouTube: there are a number of videos, some with two pianists, some by a soloist; it is fascinating for children to watch the fast movement of the fingers.

A POBREZINHA	TRACK 77
Composer	Heitor Villa-Lobos
Performer	Sonia Rubinsky
Time	2'21"
Source	Naxos

Another piece from Prole do Bebê in which the rag doll is pictured as a floppy, well-worn but much loved toy.

Key Words

Dynamic(s)
A term used in music for the volume of sound.

Handsigns
Handsigns are hand-formed shapes that correlate with the singing-names. Both are used simultaneously. Each singing-name has its own specific handsign shape, so that with constant use, the physical memory of the hand shape can prompt the aural memory with the correct pitch.

Metre
Rhythm gives rise to the feeling of pulse [heartbeat], and both together set up a sense of 'stronger' and 'less strong' beats. When performed, a piece of music will give rise to a recurring and identifiable pattern of 'strong' and 'weak' beats. For instance, a pattern of: strong-weak-weak-weak / strong-weak-weak-weak produces a metre of 4. In music notation the metre is shown as a Time Signature.

Phrase
Phrase is a portion of a melody, consisting of a group of notes that give the impression of 'belonging together'. Singers draw breath before the first note of a phrase and use that to sing the complete phrase. The melodies notated in this book are always shown with phrase marks.

Pitch
This is the melodic aspect of sound. For example, a high sounding melodic note is high in pitch; a low sounding melodic note is low in pitch.

Pulse [heartbeat]
Pulse and beat are usually interchangeable terms.

When patterns of rhythm are performed, a regular sensation of pulse can be felt.

For the purposes of First Steps into Music, pulse is treated as being the 'live' sensation of the music, the heartbeat, so to speak. When performing a song or listening to music, this heartbeat may be shown through, for example, gently tapping the chest.

The word 'beat' on its own can be useful for describing what has been or will be experienced when singing a song. So, for example, 'phrase 1 is eight beats long and phrase 2 is four beats long.'

Rhythm
Rhythm is the 'river' of music. It flows from beginning to end on a continuous tide of sound and sometimes silence. The pattern of longer and shorter sounds in songs largely mimics the pattern of the words in the text, poem or rhyme.

Rhythm names
These are names that help children to develop skills and understanding about rhythm. In this book, ta and teh-teh are used, and are specific to two basic elements of rhythm. Because they are spoken names, children find that what they have sung and tapped can be easily identified by using the rhythm names, and that these in turn are a useful intermediary step to reading and writing rhythm notation.

Singing-names [Solfa]
These are the names of melodic notes which singers can find very helpful. They are more usually known by the collective name of Solfa. The names, for example, soh [s], me [m], lah [l], can be used by singers to understand the relationship between sounds of different pitch, and over a period of time assist them in developing a useful music reading ability.

The most common solfa names in order of ascending pitch are:

doh [d] ray [r] me [m] fah [f] soh [s] lah [l] te [t]

This series of seven pitch names is repeated successively for sounds of yet higher and lower pitch, eg d r m f s l t d' r' m'...and so on. The mark ['] to the upper right denotes the pitch is an octave [8 notes] higher than the first d r m. If the mark [,] is to the lower right, eg d, r, m, then this denotes the pitch is an octave lower than the first d r m.

Tempo
This is the rate of pace at which the pulse [heartbeat] moves.

Timbre
This word is used when speaking of the tone-colour or characteristic quality of sound. Timbre enables the ear to distinguish the difference between, say, a child, woman and man singing the same song.

The CD

Song Index

TITLE	TRACK
A sailor went to sea, sea, sea	1
Bounce high, bounce low	2
Bow, wow, wow	3
Button you must wander	4
Can you tap this rhythm?	5
Can you tap your shoulders?	6
Charlie over the ocean	7
Chest, chest, knee, toe	8
Copy me	9
Doggie, doggie	10
Down came Andrew	11
Down the road	12
Early in the morning	13
Engine, engine	14
Five little monkeys	15
Follow my leader	16
Glowing candlelight	17
Going on a picnic	18
Have you brought?	19
Hello, how are you?	20
Here comes a bluebird	21
Here comes Mrs Macaroni	22
Here I come	23
Here is the beehive	24
Here sits a fat cat	25
Here we go Looby Loo	26
Hey, hey, look at me	27
Hickety tickety	28
How many miles to Babylon?	29
I have a dog	30
I have lost the cupboard key	31
I, I, me oh my	32
I see you	33
Ickle, ockle	34
Jack in the box	35
Jelly on a plate	36
Listen, listen, here I come	37
Little Johnny dances	38
Little Sally Saucer	39
Lots of rosy apples	40
Mice, mice	41
Miss, miss	42
On a log	43
Once a man fell in a well	44
Peter taps with one hammer	45
Pitter, patter	46
Rain is falling down	47
Rain on the green grass	48
Rain, rain, go away	49
Round and round the village	50
Sally go round the sun	51
Snail, snail	52
Spinning top	53
Starlight, star bright	54
Suo gân	55
There was a man	56
Three little birds	57
Tick, tock, see our clock	58
Touch your shoulders	59
Who has the penny?	60
Willum he had seven sons	61

Listening Material index

COMPOSER	TITLE	TIME	TRACK
Bucalossi	The Grasshopper's Dance	3'50"	62
Daquin	Le Coucou [Pièces de clavecin Book 1]	2'13"	63
Hertel/Lanchbery	Clog Dance [La fille mal gardée]	2'11"	64
Grieg	In the Hall of the Mountain King [Peer Gynt]	2'40"	65
Bizet	La Toupie [The Top] [Jeux d'enfants]	1'01"	66
Kodály	The Viennese Musical Clock [Háry János]	2'06"	67
Shatin	Nun, Gimel, Hei, Shin	2'15"	68
Britten	Oliver Cromwell	0'45"	69
Fučík	Entry of the Gladiators [Triumphal March]	2'59"	70
Handel	The Arrival of the Queen of Sheba [Solomon]	3'06"	71
Ibert	Parade [Divertissement]	2'00"	72
Mussorgsky [Ravel]	Bydło [Pictures at an Exhibition]	3'17"	73
Rimsky-Korsakov	Flight of the Bumble Bee [The Tale of the Tsar Saltan]	1'34"	74
Anderson	The Typewriter	1'43"	75
Villa-Lobos	O Polichinelo [Punch]	0'52"	76
Villa-Lobos	A Pobrezinha [The rag doll]	2'21"	77

The Songs

The recordings are intended to help the teacher learn the melodies of the songs. Before teaching a song to the children, the teacher will need to be familiar enough with the tune and words (at least verse 1, if there are several verses) and to teach it, ideally from memory. Therefore, each song recording features just the melody and words of one verse and is sung at the pitch to be found in the printed version.

The Listening Material

There is a separate introduction to this item. See page 159. The Teaching Ideas in the Units will identify when an item can be helpful in the teaching.

Unit Checklist

The Unit Checklist to be found on page 24 can be downloaded from the CD.

Planning Template

The printed version of the template on page 20 can also be downloaded.

The Rhythm Cards

These provide visual reading material for the children and can be downloaded and printed as laminated cards or projected on to a white screen. The Units will tell the teacher when they are to be used as a teaching tool.

Addressing the 2014 National Curriculum for Music

Specifically devised for schoolteachers in England and Wales and included as an additional resource, this guide highlights the key requirements in Music Programmes of Study from September 2014. It indicates how **First Steps: Age 5-7** supports the aims generally for Key Stage 1, also listing detailed examples from various Units throughout the handbook.